THE INVINCIBLE CROSS

THE INVINCIBLE CROSS

A Rediscovery of the Meaning of Atonement

FRANK H. CRUMPLER

WORD BOOKS
PUBLISHER
WACO, TEXAS

THE INVINCIBLE CROSS

ISBN 0–8499–0023–9
Library of Congress Catalog Card Number: 77–83322

Printed in the United States of America

Scripture quotations marked KJV are from the King James Version of the Bible; all others are from the Revised Standard Version of the Bible, copyrighted 1946, 1952 © 1971, 1973 by the Division of Christian Education of the National Council of Churches of Christ in the U.S.A., and are used by permission.

Poems on pp. 59 and 99 are from *Masterpieces of Religious Verse*. Reprinted by permission of Harper & Row, Publishers.

To Glenda—
co-laborer, fellow-pilgrim
on the glorious journey, my most helpful critic,
mother of our three precious children—
my beloved wife

CONTENTS

PREFACE

The cross of Christ is the symbol of divine love and sacrifice which stands at the heart of the Christian gospel. From the earliest days of Christianity Christ's death and resurrection have been regarded as a mid-point of human history. The events which preceded his death are seen as preparation for it, all that followed has been interpreted as a result. Christianity derives its name from Christ, but its deepest meaning comes from the cross. It would be impossible then to understand the nature and meaning of the Christian faith without thoroughly understanding the doctrine of the atonement. Reduced to its simplest definition, Christianity is "Jesus Christ and him crucified." The gospel indeed is a person—Jesus Christ our Lord.

Christianity was born in a time of confusion and chaos. There is a strong parallel between the times of Jesus and the times in which we live. Take away the technological and scientific advances of the last two thousand years, and you will find mankind is pretty much the same today as when Christ walked the earth. Man's hopes, dreams and aspirations have not changed a great deal. There is the same frantic search for inner peace and security that people of every generation have felt. It is amid this kind of turbulence in life that the cross is most at home. Certainly it is here and now that the cross in all its majestic power should be understood, appreciated and responded to.

The word *invincible* is defined "incapable of being overcome or subdued." When applied to the cross of Christ the word *invincible* is most significant, because it describes an outstanding characteristic of the cross. The passing of time has neither diminished nor overcome the power of Christ's death. History provides abundant evidence of this truth. Across the past twenty centuries nations have risen to power and collapsed; movements have been started and have been forgotten; men of great power have emerged to dominate the scene of human activity, but have also faded into oblivion. But from the earliest days until the present, the ups and downs of nineteen hundred years have not diminished even one bit of the power and glory of the cross of Christ. The cross is truly invincible.

As our beginning point, we will examine the cross historically and prophetically; that is, we will examine how the cross stands in history and see that its place in the unfolding of human events is adequately supported by prophetic passages from the Old Testament. Next, we will examine the cross in the light of its relationships to man and to God. In a third section, we will study the idea of faith as it is related to the atoning work of Jesus Christ on the cross. In part four we will examine the significance of the doctrine of the atonement in the writings and ministry of the Apostle Paul, with special emphasis on the necessity and urgency of proclaiming the gospel in the last quarter of the twentieth century.

This is intended to be a presentation of many aspects of the doctrine of the atonement. It is, in every sense, a serious effort to help make the doctrine of the atonement come alive through a reexamination of some basic ideas concerning the invincible cross. There is a great deal of mystery about the cross. We confess at the outset that some of the mysteries concerning the cross must ever remain mysteries. The human mind cannot fathom all the depths of God's love, mercy, justice, and grace symbolized in Christ's death and resurrection. Some of the most wonderful truths connected with the cross defy description or explanation. Perhaps as we examine this great doctrine of the church more closely, some new insight or fresh understanding might be gained. Or perhaps some familiar truth might come into new focus and with a different perspective. May God grant that the discovery of some new thought about the invincible cross will strengthen your understanding and add to your faith.

Part 1

THE PERSPECTIVE
OF THE CROSS

I

THE CROSS AND
HISTORY

*There was a cross in the heart of
God before there was one planted on
a green hill outside Jerusalem.*
Charles Allen Dinsmore

And all who dwell on earth will worship it, everyone whose name has not been written before the foundation of the world in the book of life of the Lamb that was slain (Rev. 13:8).

There can be no repetition of Calvary, only echoes. The crucifixion of Christ is a historical event, but it is infinitely more—it is an event in eternity. God moves in a realm which is beyond time. It is infinite—without beginning and without end. In the coming of Jesus into the world, eternity came into time and, therefore, the Christ-event belongs to infinity and to the finite—to the timeless and to time. This is precisely why Christ belongs to every age and why he is always contemporary. As a person, Christ lived in human history. As the eternal God, he is a present reality, daily confronting mankind.

One of the most beautiful symbols of Christ in early Christian art was the picture of a lamb. The lamb appears to have been slain; the closed eyes, the riven side and the blood which is visible just above all four hoofs offer evidence that the lamb has already been put to death. And yet the lamb is standing. The very fact that the lamb stands erect gives evidence of life. So this picture is a simple illustration of a mighty truth: Christ has been put to death, yet he is alive! Christ is both the victim and the victor. This is true because Christ became the link between eternity and time.

The cross was an event in history; Christ was crucified on a specific cross, on a given day, at an exact place. Yet if we are to understand the true meaning of his death, we must see it as a part of eternity. This is why John spoke of him as "the Lamb slain from the foundation of the world" (Rev. 13:8, KJV). From God's point of view, Christ had already been crucified when he spoke the world into being, although the crucifixion did not take place historically until Jesus died on a Roman cross outside Jerusalem. Emil Brunner was exactly right when he said that this event of Jesus' death does not belong to the historical plane. It is superhistory, history which lies in a dimension no his-

torian knows, insofar as he is a mere historian.[1] This
does not mean that the death of Christ is less significant, but that it is timeless as a part of the eternal
divine order. The cross and all that it means had already taken place in the heart and mind of God from
the beginning. All of God's dealing with his creation
moves to the point of this zenith—the atonement.

THE CROSS AS PAST EVENT

God is always present in history, moving in his creation. The way we respond to that fact depends on our
belief in God and in his activity. One who believes in
God can see evidences of his presence and power everywhere. Yet one who does not believe in God will not
accept anything as evidence of his activity. God breaks
into the course of human history from time to time.
Sometimes he works through startling and miraculous
deeds which seem to alter the course of natural events.
Nowhere is this seen more clearly than in the miraculous birth, crucifixion and resurrection of Jesus. Christ,
the God-man, became the Lamb of sacrifice, and in his
death the eternal reality of God became a historical
event. This, of course, is in keeping with God's eternal
redemptive purpose. In Christ the forgiveness and salvation of God was made available to all mankind. This
truth is so aptly stated by Charles Dinsmore, who said
there was a cross in the heart of God before there was
one planted on a green hill outside Jerusalem. Christ
died thousands of years before he came to earth; he
died in the heart and mind of God.

Now, naturally the question arises, "Why did the
crucifixion take place when it did?" There is no easy
answer to a question like that, but our answer does not
have to be based entirely upon speculation. First, let
us consider the fact that God had been at work since

the beginning of his creation setting the stage of history for the coming of Christ. The Apostle Paul mentions in Galatians 4:4, "But when the time had fully come, God sent forth his Son." God's choice of timing had to do with the flow of human events. A close examination of the times of Jesus will reveal that circumstances were exactly right for the spread of the gospel through the Middle Eastern world. The conquering Romans had provided a common language for preaching the gospel everywhere. The *Pax Romana* had provided safety on the high seas, allowing Christians as well as others to travel unharmed. This fact alone accounts for the very rapid spread of the good news of Jesus Christ by his apostles into distant lands.

The phrase, "when the time had fully come," includes a multitude of conditions and circumstances which had to be set in order before the birth of Christ. God waited until the human family was ready for the Christ-event. Even then, they crucified the Lord of life. Mankind was hardly able, even after so many centuries of sacrifices, to accept a sacrifice once for all. Members of the human family were not even then prepared to accept the fact that life comes out of death, that victory comes out of surrender, that their Messiah could have a kingdom "not of this world." This is why the phrase, "When the time had fully come, God sent forth his Son," is so important.

With such stress on the eternal nature of the atonement, it might seem that we are trying to minimize the historical aspect. This is not the case at all. We must still see the importance of the crucifixion as a historical act. The cross was necessary in its historical form, within the flow of human history. It is an expression of God's nature made visible and tangible in a historical perspective. How else could mankind know of the love of God? God meets man on the plane of his own existence. There was nothing mythical nor theoretical about it. The cross on which Christ died was a rough, heavy, cruel cross. The physical pain he experienced was also real. The insults of the angry mob were strong and biting. He endured the real and unbearable agony of suffering in order to accomplish the plan and purpose of the infinite God. Thus, the cross takes its place in the historical progression of mankind. The death of Christ upon it constitutes an event in history. But the crucifixion of Christ is also a present and contemporary event, just as if Christ had died on the cross this very day.

THE CROSS AS PRESENT REALITY

Christ became God's perfect sacrifice for the sins of the world. Since this is true, let's think for a moment about the nature of sacrifice. The system of sacrifice in the Old Testament seems constantly to have been revised and reformed. The sacrifices of the past were not effective for one's present sins and for that reason the sacrifices were offered again and again. But when Christ came and died on the cross he became the sacrifice which ended all other sacrifices. The offering of this Lamb was supreme. It was far-reaching. It was enough to last forever. And so, ever-new and ever-effective, the death of the Son of God moves with the stream of history as if Jesus had died this very morning. It is vital, then, to understand the reality of the cross for the present. Our Lord's atoning death has been contemporary for every generation since the beginning of man. This underscores the fact that the cross of Jesus is invincible beyond our comprehension.

The Christian gospel is both simple and profound. It is simple enough to say we believe that God came and revealed himself in and through Jesus Christ. Yet our personal obligation comes into sharp focus when we understand that God, who came in the person of Jesus Christ, has given himself freely in our place. It is true that he who knew no sin became sin for us. In order to bring about forgiveness and reconciliation, God allowed the sinless Christ to be crucified in our place. He was our substitute—our sin offering. The obedient Son of God bore the burden of the world's transgression. Paul put it so beautifully in his letter to the Corinthians: "For our sake he made him to be sin who knew no sin, so that in him we might become the righteousness of God" (2 Cor. 5:21). This is the greatest fact in all history—that Jesus Christ died to save all who would believe in him and obey him. This truth is as real in this present moment as it was when it was first announced. Look at the cross once again through the word picture of John Newton's beautiful hymn, "He Died For Me."

> I saw one hanging on a tree,
>   In agony and blood;
> He fixed his languid eyes on me,
>   As near his cross I stood.
>
> Oh, can it be upon a tree
>   The Saviour died for me?
> My soul is thrilled, my heart
>   is still
> To think He died for me! [2]

THE CROSS AS ETERNAL HOPE

God was strangely at work on Calvary. We stand in awe at the very thought of the eternal significance of this execution. It is uniquely the Lord's work, not man's. The Jews were not willing to accept the fact that mercy and grace can flow out of judgment, but the

only way we will ever understand the cross is to see it
in terms of God's never-ending love for his creation.
Jesus did not come to be ministered unto but to minister and to give his life a ransom for many (Mark
10:45).

This act of Christ on the cross is unique because it is
an event both in time and in eternity. We see him as a
good man who was put to death, but God sees him as
an eternal sacrifice. D. M. Baillie reminds us that while
some generations look forward to the cross and others
look back to it as an event in time, God's view of the
cross is as if it is happening right now.[3] In every age
God is reaching out like a loving father to embrace his
wayward and estranged children. He stands ever-willing
to lift the load of sin from his people. Such suffering
in the heart of God and such longing for reconciliation
with mankind defies description.

In that sense, Christ's agony upon the cross still goes
on. His is a suffering that continues as long as there is
a single heart or life that has not been touched by his
sacrifice. His agony will continue in the heart of God
until the end of the world, until the kingdoms of this
world have become the kingdoms of our God. The
offering of Christ, says E. Y. Mullins, was indeed an
eternal atonement in the sense that it was an expression
of an eternal impulse of God's love, an eternal desire
to give himself for the good of his creatures, and also
in the sense that it is eternally efficacious.[4]

Divine sacrifice did not begin at Calvary, but it is
there we see its most glorious expression. Against the
background of what seems to be tragedy, the greatest of
all victories was won. Out of this setting—the cross, the
crowd, the crucified—the end of one life was made the
beginning of life for those who believe. The cross of
wood on which Jesus was nailed was but an earthly
symbol of an eternal cross which is in the heart and

mind of God.[5] God had the cross in his infinite plan
from the beginning of time, for Christ is indeed "the
Lamb of God slain from the foundation of the world"
(Rev. 13:8, KJV).

William Manson says:

> "He who accepts the cross does so in the spirit
> of 'Father, forgive them, for they know not what
> they do.' Face to face with the event on Calvary,
> we have to give ourselves account finally of what
> is involved in real forgiveness. . . . All forgiveness
> is a faint derivitive of the supreme act of
> God." [6]

More than nineteen centuries have rolled by since
the cross of Christ was set up on Golgotha. Even
though we are prone to think of this as an isolated his-
toric event, it has great eternal significance. It is a part
of God's plan for the forgiveness of mankind. These
two basic elements—the historical and the eternal—
should always remain together. One should not detract
from the importance of the other. We need to keep in
mind the truth that the atonement was and is within
the life of God as well as within the history of man.
The atonement is uniquely his. The cross, with all its
meaning, was made necessary by his judgment and
made possible by his love. He alone can apply the
meaning of the cross to each generation. He is the Lamb
eternally slain, but standing. His cross becomes a bridge
uniting time and eternity. The sacrifice of Christ is
still going on. Our Lamb of sacrifice is still slain and
suffering for the sins of his estranged creation. Christ
is still waiting for man to decide to give him his rightful
place as Lord and Master.

II

THE CROSS AND
PROPHECY

Ere he raised the lofty mountains,
Formed the sea or built the sky,
Love eternal, free and boundless
Forced the Lord of life to die,
Lifted up the Prince of princes
On the throne of Calvary.
                    —Welsh Hymn

That it might be fulfilled which was spoken by the prophet, They parted my garments among them, and upon my vesture did they cast lots (Matt. 27:35, KJV).

The Old Testament is the strong foundation upon which the superstructure of the New Testament stands. The New Testament both explains and gives a record of the fulfillment of the Old Testament. The utterances of the prophets cannot be ignored in a thorough study of the doctrine of the atonement. God revealed himself to man through Jesus Christ, the Word made flesh. The strange thing about this is that those in whose midst the Christ-event took place were those who had heard beforehand the word spoken through the prophets concerning the Messiah. God had given such revelation concerning man's sin and the coming of the Messiah that it is hard to realize that the contemporaries of Jesus actually rejected him.

The confession of Jesus as the Messiah was initially made against a backdrop of first century Judaism. It was characteristic of the Jews that their forms of thought were religious rather than philosophical.[1] Unlike the Greeks, whose thought patterns and insights were shaped by philosophy, the Jews interpreted their universe in terms of their religious experience and traditions. The Jewish view of the universe was clothed in the dramatic expressions which are natural to religion. All that happened or existed or was felt was interpreted by the Jewish mind as part of the will and purpose of God, the almighty personal Creator and Ruler. It was to men and women who had this religious background that the gospel was proclaimed. In this setting the message was first heard, "God was in Christ reconciling the world to himself. . . . we beseech you on behalf of Christ, be reconciled to God" (2 Cor. 5:19–20).

It was through the prophets that God began to prepare the way for the coming of the Deliverer and Messiah, Jesus Christ. As we go back to these prophetic utterances, we can see the entire plan of God unfolding. God has dealt with man since the creation according to a divine plan. God's activity is not being made up as we go along, but always follows a prescribed plan which he is always seeking to reveal to mankind. God wants to reveal himself. He always has. He revealed himself in nature. He revealed himself in wind, smoke, fire, and hundreds of other expressions of his presence. But, the greatest and fullest revelation of himself came to us in and through Jesus Christ. God discloses his love and compassion in the cross.

The unveiling of his true nature through Jesus Christ was begun when he opened the eyes of the prophets to see what others of their day had not seen and to "tell forth" what he had revealed to them. The prophets of the Jewish religion place much emphasis on true repentance and personal righteousness. This is especially true of Amos, Hosea, and Isaiah. So great is their stress on personal piety that one might think good works have some positive share in the attainment of forgiveness.[2] It is true, however, that in the writings of the early prophets the attainment of forgiveness has a unique relationship with personal piety. Forgiveness and righteousness are never separate in Old Testament prophecy; they are always considered parts of the same unity.

EARLY REFERENCES

The history of the redemptive relationship between Jehovah and his people is recorded in the Old Testament. The promise of redemption runs like a golden thread throughout the fabric of the Old Testament.

The first mention of Christ is the statement God made to the serpent when Adam and Eve sinned in the Garden of Eden. It appears as both a prophecy and a promise, and certainly one which was not fully understood by the hearers. After God had pronounced a curse upon the serpent, he said:

> I will put enmity between you and the woman,
>   and between your seed and her seed;
> he shall bruise your head,
>   and you shall bruise his heel. (Gen. 3:15).

This verse towers like a mountain peak in the book of Genesis. It reveals two outstanding features of the Messiah. First, it alludes to Christ's sufferings for and because of sin. Here is the note of prophecy which obviously gives the great war drama of salvation significance beyond the human race. It is the announcement of enmity between Christ and Satan. But there is another aspect to the verse—that of promise. The promise is of no small importance; it stands for the comfort and edification of the people of God in every generation. Perhaps a little more explanation of this verse would be in order here.

By the words, "your seed and her seed," God meant the seed of the serpent, which is sin, and the seed of the woman, who is Christ. Satan would damage Christ ("you shall bruise his heel"), but Christ would destroy the power of Satan ("he shall bruise your head"). To "bruise the head" is a picture of fatal and final destruction. To "bruise the heel" is a picture of damage which is neither fatal nor final. Thus Christ is victorious over the power of darkness, even though he suffers the agony of the cross unto death. On the cross, Satan "bruised the heel" of Christ by causing him physical suffering and death. Yet, death could not hold him. He arose from the tomb, having paid the price for our salvation. By doing this Christ had destroyed Satan's power forever. This is what is meant by "he shall bruise

your head." The true believer shares in this victory
with Christ.

<h2>Messianic Concept</h2>

The Messiah is the person through whom God's
kingdom is established upon the earth. Throughout the
Old Testament we find an ever-increasing hope of a
personal deliverer, and this hope seems to be inseparable from the life of the nation. God had promised
deliverance and the Old Testament Jews cherished the
expectation of complete deliverance through the Messiah. In a physical sense, the Jews expected final triumph over their enemies, but in a specific way they
held on to the hope of personal and individual redemption which was promised to them in the covenant. In
Exodus 6:7 God had said, "I will take you for my
people, and I will be your God." It was on the grounds
of this promise that the prophets, while pronouncing
judgment upon the sins of the people, never lost sight
of the day of salvation and redemption ahead. The
name *Messiah* is used in a double sense, to describe the
great hope of a glorious future for the nation, and to
describe the hope of a personal Messiah who is to be
the key figure in the perfected kingdom.

The Messiah in the Old Testament is pictured as a
king. Through him God could work out his saving
purpose because he was the head of the nation. All
through the history of Israel we find the idea that
Jehovah raised up certain individuals to lead his people.
It was only by his power that the king was qualified for
the righteous government of the people. Also, by his
power the leaders and the people could become victorious over all their enemies.

The messianic concept reaches a high point in the
writing of Isaiah, as we shall see later on. Micah,

Isaiah's younger contemporary, emphasizes the humble
origin of the future messianic ruler. Micah also indicates that the messiah will be of the lineage of David.

> But you, O Bethlehem Ephrathah,
> who are little to be among the clans of Judah,
> from you shall come forth for me
> one who is to be ruler in Israel,
> whose origin is from of old,
> from ancient days (Mic. 5:2).

ISAIAH'S PROPHECY

Isaiah was the first of the prophets to refer to a
king-deliverer who would come at some future time.
He was by far the most outstanding prophet of the
eighth century B.C. Through Isaiah, God revealed much
of his purpose for the world. The prophet was more
than a spiritual giant; he possessed a keen insight and
a depth of understanding which set him apart from
his contemporaries.

Amos was foretelling a time when the shattered for-
tunes of Judah would be restored (Amos 9:11).
Hosea, who was also preaching in the Northern Kingdom, looked forward to the reunion of the two kingdoms under David's line (Hos. 3:5). Yet, in the
thought of Isaiah, the personality of the king is brought
into focus. Thus, we are presented with a more significant mention of a unique personal ruler who would
bring special glory to David's house. "Therefore the
Lord himself will give you a sign. Behold, a young
woman shall conceive and bear a son, and shall call
his name Immanuel" (Isa. 7:14).

The prophet's lofty vision reaches beyond Judah's
distress to the time of Judah's deliverance. It is to
Isaiah that the revelation is given of a true king—
Immanuel, "a God who is with us"—who would arise

out of the house of David and deliver Israel. This passage is one of the most difficult in the entire Old Testament to interpret. The certainty of God's promised deliverance will be signified by the birth of a child who will be the embodiment of God. The significance of the prophecy is not in the mystery of his birth so much as it is in the mystery of his personality (Immanuel—God is with us) and in the pledge of victory and deliverance of which his birth is to be a sign.

Isaiah refers to Immanuel as a ruler of the land in other passages (Isa. 8:8). He definitely continues the parallelism of the line of thought in the prophecy in Isaiah 9:6–7. In this scripture he reveals the identity of Immanuel with four descriptive names and the role of deliverer-king of the line of David:

> For to us a child is born,
>   to us a son is given;
> and the government will be upon his shoulder,
>   and his name will be called
> "Wonderful Counselor, Mighty God,
>   Everlasting Father, Prince of Peace."
> Of the increase of his government and of peace
>   there will be no end,
> upon the throne of David, and over his kingdom,
>   to establish it, and to uphold it
> with justice and with righteousness
>   from this time forth and for evermore.
> The zeal of the Lord of hosts will do this.

The titles "Wonderful Counselor," "Mighty God," "Everlasting Father," "Prince of Peace" indicate that the Messiah and King will be the instrument of God's deliverance of his people. He will possess perfect wisdom and power and will exercise over his people a fatherly and peaceful rule forever. This idea of the

Messiah of the house of David is continued in Isaiah 11:2:

> And the spirit of the Lord shall rest upon him,
>   the spirit of wisdom and understanding,
>   the spirit of counsel and might,
>   the spirit of knowledge and the fear of the Lord.

Here, the attributes with which he is endowed by the "Spirit of the Lord" are those which qualify him for the perfect discharge of royal functions. So numerous are the references to the Messiah in Isaiah's prophecy, we shall list these references with corresponding New Testament passages which indicate the fulfillment of these prophecies:

OLD TESTAMENT	PROPHECY	FULFILLED
Isaiah 7:14	"Virgin Birth"	Matthew 1:18 Luke 1:26–35
Isaiah 9:1–2	"Ministry in Galilee"	Matthew 4:12–16
Isaiah 53:3	"Rejected by Jews"	John 1:11, 5:43 Luke 4:29, 4:17–25 Luke 23:18
Isaiah 62:11	"Triumphal Entry"	John 12:13, 14 Matthew 21:1–11 John 12:12
Isaiah 50:6	"Smitten, Spat Upon"	Mark 14:65 Mark 15:17 John 19:1–3, 18:22
Isaiah 53:4–5	"Suffered"	Matthew 8:16, 17 Romans 4:25 1 Cor. 15:3

Isaiah 53:12   "Crucified"   Matthew 27:38
                                        Mark 15:27–28
                                        Luke 23:33

Isaiah 53:9   "Buried with the rich" Matthew 27:57–60

Who could deny that God's plan for the redemption of the world is revealed in Isaiah's prophecy? As one glances over the many passages which point forward to the promised Messiah, the divine pattern of his life and death become more obvious. Fulfilled in their every detail, these Old Testament passages are but shadows of the New Testament record. The incomparable and indestructible plan of God was perfectly wrought in history. To this the New Testament record bears irrefutable evidence. The most minute details of the life, death and resurrection of Christ are the confirmation and fulfillment of some earlier prophecies.

PROPHETIC PSALMS

The idea of sacrifice is of major significance in the Psalms. The psalmist also devotes an abundance of comments to the specific sacrifice of the Lamb of God. In the Psalms we find a new emphasis on the real relationship between sacrifice and obedience (Ps. 40:6–8); without obedience, sacrifices are worthless and repugnant to God. The death of Jesus Christ upon the cross can also be found in key passages in the Psalms. The idea of the Suffering Servant also appears. Such psalms as Psalm 22 constitute a key to understanding the work of Christ that unifies the entire revelation of God's dealing with human sins. Yet it is remarkable that such a conception of the way of atonement was very far from the average Jewish mind when Jesus came. In no sense can the New Testament doctrine of the atonement be said to be the product of the thought and spirit of the times. The prophets only laid the foundation in thought forms and in religious atmosphere for the atonement of Christ.

The following passages from the Psalms indicate a prophetic mood which obviously forecast the circumstances surrounding our Lord's crucifixion. Even though many of these prophetic fragments seem to be trivial, Christ fulfilled each one through his actual suffering and death. Not even the smallest detail connected with the death of Christ can be considered unimportant. Therefore, these are not to be ignored as a part of the Old Testament prediction of the Christ's sacrifice on the cross.

OLD TESTAMENT	PROPHECY	FULFILLED
Psalm 22:8	"Prophetic words"	Matthew 27:43
Psalm 22:6–8	"Mocked"	Matthew 27:39–44 Mark 15:29–32
Psalm 22:16	"Pierced"	John 20:27
Psalm 27:12	"False witnesses"	Matthew 26:60, 61
Psalm 35:11	"Silent"	Matthew 26:62, 63
Psalm 38:13–14	"No Word Spoken"	Matthew 27:12–14
Psalm 41:9	"Betrayed by Friends"	Mark 14:10 Matthew 26:14–16
Psalm 34:20	"No bone broken"	John 19:33
Psalm 22:18	"Soldiers cast lots"	Mark 15:24
Psalm 69:4	"Hated without cause"	John 15:23–25

Psalm 69:21	"Gall and vinegar"	John 19:29
		Matthew 27:34, 48
Psalm 110:4	"Like Melchizedek"	Hebrews 5:5, 6

The prophet wrote with tremendous insight, for each idea he expressed finds fulfillment in the New Testament. The ties between the old and the new cannot be denied.

It is obvious that these psalms were familar to Jesus. We may be sure that the many references Jesus made to the psalms were not coincidental. He recognized in the psalms the expression of the religious experience of his people, and at the same time he saw in them his own ministry and passion.

Eric Routley, in his excellent little book *Ascent to the Cross,* points out very adequately that Christ knew something of the agony that was ahead for him, because of his familiarity with the prophecies of the Old Testament.[3]

Part 2

THE RELATIONSHIPS
OF THE CROSS

III

THE CROSS AND SATAN

Found now at Golgotha
  dwarfing the hill
The horrifying hate-carved tree
  where God hung still.
Yet, beautiful this tree of life
  grows to me,
this blood, this cross, where I
  too die and taste eternity.
                    Elliot Knight

And when they came to a place called Golgotha (which means the place of a skull), they offered him wine to drink, mingled with gall; but when he tasted it, he would not drink it. And when they had crucified him, they divided his garments among them by casting lots; then they sat down and kept watch over him there (Matt. 27:33–36).

The New Testament does not give us all the details of our Lord's agony on the cross. No doubt it is better that we have so few details of his actual suffering. You see, it is impossible for a Christian to think about the cross without becoming emotionally involved. How could the gospel writers describe fully each detail of his crucifixion without making such a description sound degrading and demeaning. Anyway, words can never convey the full meaning of this event, could not describe it adequately. Thus, the gospel writers tell us *what* happened without spending many words in telling us *how* it happened. Luke simply says "And when they came to the place which is called The Skull, there they crucified him." (Luke 23:33). Yet these few words convey all the heartache, agony and triumph connected with the death of our Lord. These few words are enough: "There they crucified him." In these words we can hear angry shouting, painful groans, blows of the hammer upon the nails, the dead thud of the cross as it drops into its place. "There they crucified him." Somehow that's all that needs to be said, for the imagination, guided by the Holy Spirit, can supply all of the details that are not spelled out in the Gospel records. It is the fact that Jesus died that has become the central fact in the drama of redemption.

THE ETERNAL CONFLICT

The scriptures describe Jesus as being in constant conflict with Satan. The Book of Mark tells us of Jesus' temptation. "Temptation" is a poor translation of *peirazō*. The Greek word is open to two interpretations: one, an eternal movement toward evil, wrong, subjective desire—truly temptation; or two, an attack from outside, a fiery ordeal, a test or trial thrust upon one by an enemy. It is the latter view that fits here. Jesus is not tempted. He is attacked! [1]

In Mark 1 we find hints of the cosmic struggle between God and Satan. Jesus is said to "cast out devils" and to heal those with "unclean spirits." In verse 24 Satan's struggle with Jesus is suggested: "Let *us* alone." J. B. Phillips, in his book, *Your God Is Too Small,* says, "Christ definitely spoke of a power of spiritual evil and, using the language of his contemporaries, he called this power Satan. Christ does not fully explain the origin or power of Satan, but he does recognize "evil as evil, not as a mere absence of good. He did, whenever possible, destroy it." [2]

When Satan has power over a life, sin has dominion. John Calvin defined original sin as "hereditary depravity and corruption of our nature, diffused through all the parts of the soul, rendering us subject to the Divine wrath, and producing in us those works which the Scriptures call 'works of the flesh.' " [3] It was the belief of that day, shared by Jesus and the church, that death was not a sweet release sent by God but was instead an enemy, the last great enemy, a weapon of Satan.[4]

Hebrews 2:14 says, "Since therefore the children share in flesh and blood, he himself likewise partook of the same nature, that through death he might destroy him who has the power of death [that is, the devil]." In the cross Jesus proves himself victorious over sin, death, and Satan. The conflict between God and Satan comes to a climax in the cross of Christ.

"Here light and darkness, holiness and sin, God and the devil come into deadly combat. Holiness and truth here forever conquered sin and evil." [5]

THE CORRESPONDING ATTITUDES

Satan's tools on earth are human attitudes such as intolerance, materialism, selfishness, and violence. With these he fights his battle with Christ; these atti-

tudes in people helped crucify Christ and continue to
work against God's plan today.

Intolerance

A part of the guilt of crucifixion must be attributed
to intolerance. We can see this attitude represented in
the religious leaders of Jesus' day—the Pharisees,
scribes and the lawyers. They were intolerant of the
new spirit Jesus gave to religion. They were more concerned about the "mint, anise and cummin" of religion
than the love and kindness of which Jesus spoke. That
kind of attitude makes provisions for getting the ox
out of the ditch, but none for lifting the suffering
brother-man who has fallen. Jesus came preaching a
message which was intended to add a glorious crown
to all they had been teaching, but they were blinded
by bigotry and intolerance and would have none of it.
Christ's gentleness angered them. His brushing aside
of false ideas by his quiet "But I say unto you" moved
them to frenzy. These religious leaders demonstrated
all that betrays, deadens and crucifies.

The same spirit of intolerance is still evident today
and it still emanates a killing influence wherever it is
found. Nothing can kill the real spirit and meaning of
Christ's death more than religious intolerance. The
way of Christ is seen in giving every man the same
privileges we expect for ourselves. Jesus would have
us give every new idea a chance before we condemn
it. Our Lord would have us accept those with whom
we disagree in the spirit of love and understanding.
Belonging to him involves being filled with that kind
of tolerance and love.

Materialism

In reality, materialism also helped to crucify Jesus.

The money changers in the temple—the sellers of doves for sacrifices and those who changed Roman coins into Jewish sheckles for a price—embody this idea. Annas and Caiaphas who consented to the materialistic traffic in the temple, the traders who made the temple their place to buy, sell or swap goods—all these are party to his death. Greed which cannot be satisfied, desire for more and more, lust for profit and the urge to make religion a business are the expressions of the attitude that put Jesus to death. Materialism knocks at the door of the temple still bidding Christ to take the walk to Calvary again.

At one time St. Francis of Assisi was being shown through the beautiful St. Peter's Basilica in Rome. His companion remarked "No longer can the church say 'silver and gold have I none'." "No," answered Francis, "nor can she say 'in the name of Jesus, rise up and walk.' "

Selfishness

Do we find a personality in the drama of the crucifixion who typifies self-interest? Yes. It is Pontius Pilate. Selfishness must bear a part of the guilt for Jesus' execution. Pilate put self first and allowed himself to become the victim of public opinion. He thought that by crucifying Jesus he might gain an advantage for himself.

Someone has said that all sin has its origin in *pride* or self-love. If you boil pride long enough, you get pure 100 percent distilled *hatred*. Self-love becomes hate if it is given a chance to grow. Selfishness blinds the eye of the soul to real meaning, to real beauty. They tell us that fish which live in caverns finally lose their eyesight. Likewise, men who live in the dark holes of their own selfish natures lose their spiritual sight.

Visions of the loftiest, fairest, truest, and most radiant realities pass before their eyes unseen because they are blinded by selfishness.

Violence

Violence is not to be overlooked as having a share in the guilt of the crucifixion. The Roman soldiers typify this idea. To be sure, they were acting under orders and may be excused from direct guilt. Even so, the spirit of violence, always crucifies Christ. The cross is raised by the same spirit that makes mankind bent on killing. Violence and destruction are not strange to us today, nor have they ever been. The idea of "might makes right" has led many a nation and many an individual to a tragic end.

THE INEVITABLE RESULT

The forces of Satan would seem to be victorious, but it is not so. Rather, it is in death that God is finally triumphant. The real victory belonged to Christ. At this place called "Golgotha" (the place of the skull), our Lord won the greatest victory of all time. He conquered sin and Satan in life. He conquers again in death. All heaven and earth converged upon that central cross, where the great drama of redemption reached its climax. Here human sin rose up and divine love reached down and these met on that cross on Calvary. He was a King rejected, but kings and lords have knelt at his feet. Sinners nailed him to the cross, but because of his death all sinners have been invited to know his forgiveness and salvation. Death, the last enemy, had its way with him that day, but it was death who suffered defeat.

The Redeemer was victorious over sin, death and

the grave.[6] In heaven angels watched with anguish as
he suffered. In the moment of his death he cried with
a loud voice, "Father, into Thy hands I commend my
Spirit." This he said with his last breath and then ten
thousand times ten thousand voices sent up a shout
of praise to God such as no mortal ear has ever heard.
Hallelujah! The Lord God Omnipotent reigneth!
Praise Him! Glory to God in the highest! The Crucified
had become the victor. Death and the grave had suffered defeat. Heaven's door had been forever opened.
He had fulfilled the purpose for which he came into
the world. His cross was no tragedy; it was triumph!
Let us live within the brightness of that triumphant
moment. Let us march under the orders of our victorious and triumphant Lord.

IV

THE CROSS AND
GOD

Dear dying Lamb, Thy precious blood
Shall never lose its power,
Till all the ransomed Church of God
Be saved to sin no more.
            William Cowper
            "There Is a Fountain"

Behold, the Lamb of God, who takes away the sin of the world! (John 1:29).

In the cross God reveals his unending love for mankind as well as his judgment upon sin. We must allow for the plan and purpose of God in the thinking and the willing of Jesus as the Son of man. Jesus chose the cross. He had come into the world to die. He said "For this I was born, and for this I have come into the world" (John 18:37). You and I want to avoid death, and our pressing aim is to live as long as possible. Jesus is the only man who ever came into the world to die. His statement in John 10:17 makes this clear: "I lay down my life that I may take it again." There is no chance, accident or fatalism connected with his death. It was in every sense an event which followed a divine plan. He deliberately and majestically chose the cross and no one stopped the completion of God's plan. When his "hour had come," he was ready to lay down his life for the sins of the world.

THE NATURE OF GOD

The cross tells us some great secrets about the nature of God. To understand *who God is* and *what God is like* makes the drama of the crucifixion even more astounding and glorious. From Holy Scripture we see these three inseparable ideas: God, the Loving Lord, desiring the best for man; God, the Righteous Judge, condemning sin; God, the Supreme Sacrifice, enduring in himself that necessary penalty of the cross for the human family.[1] The very nature of God calls for the condemnation of sin. The cross, as a moral necessity, stands as a symbol of God's holiness and righteousness. On that cross was a demonstration of the wrath and judgment of God upon sin. Through the cross we can discover the awful and drastic nature of sin. The sinfulness of sin is revealed by the cruelty and ugliness of the cross. What suffering and shame

49

it inflicts! The horror of sin demanded the horrible death of our Lord. Again, in the words of Paul:

> "God, sending his own Son in the likeness of sinful flesh and for sin, he condemned sin in the flesh, in order that the just requirement of the law might be fulfilled in us, who walk not according to the flesh but according to the spirit." (Rom. 8:3–4)

Christ became obedient unto death in order to condemn sin on behalf of the whole human race. He tasted death of the most cruel sort. He fulfilled every detail of the law and thus removed every obstacle in the path of God's forgiveness of sin. He was in every sense the perfect Lamb of God. In mankind's long quest for God, Jesus is the climax. Jesus is God revealed to man. We learn of the nature of God as we know Jesus. What kind of God does Jesus reveal? D. M. Baillie, in his book *God Was in Christ,* says that Jesus reveals "a seeking God, whose very nature is to go the whole way into the wilderness in quest of man." [2] The New Testament teaches that man is reconciled to God through Jesus Christ. "God was in Christ reconciling the world to himself." (2 Cor. 5:9)

It was in the cross that the Son of God became also the Son of man, taking upon himself what is ours and transferring to us what is his, "so that what is his by nature becomes ours by grace." [3] John Calvin says that Jesus Christ acted as a mediator who "had to restore us to divine favor so that children of men could become children of God." [4] In Jesus Christ God provides the means whereby his ceaseless, life-giving power is perpetuated and the means of creation is revealed. A new life and a new nature is offered mankind through the person of Christ.[5]

The God of the Scriptures, Jehovah, is a merciful and gracious God. In him is the fullest expression of kindness, goodness, mercy, justice and judgment. In Jeremiah 9:24, we find that God reveals himself in this way: "Let him who glories, glory in this," says the Lord, "that he understands and knows me, that I am the Lord who practices steadfast love, justice, and righteousness in the earth." His love is the foundation of all his redemptive work, his justice is daily exercised against all sin, and his righteousness preserves and nourishes all who trust in him. God is holy; his is sovereign and absolute holiness. He is the creator, the governor and sustainer of the universe. He is the Lord of heaven and earth. He has all knowledge, all power and is limited by nothing—neither time nor space. God claims the allegiance and obedience of all his creation. He reveals himself to man as a God who hears the pleas of his creatures. He made known his ways to men of old. He declares his power through mighty acts and reveals himself in the movements of history. There is no way to measure the essence and the power of God. Reason can never comprehend God as he is. He is wholly loving and wholly just at the same time. His qualities are inseparable one from another. This is why we must see the cross in the light of all his attributes together.

Since God is absolute holiness, he cannot condone sin. He could never just pass over the disobedience of man. God could not, by the dictates of his nature, call Adam and Eve out of the fig groves and say, "Come on now and we will forget what you did this time." God's nature demanded that all sin must be paid for. This is never more clearly demonstrated than in the fact that animals were slain to provide a covering for the bodies of these two sinners. Yet, we should remember that Adam and Eve lost their innocence and were made to feel the pain of losing their position with God.

Do you see here the divine nature being satisfied and the human nature being called into reconciliation with God as a result of sin? It was necessary for the animals to be slain and for clothing to be made from their skins. It was also necessary for the disobedient ones to share in the cost of their own forgiveness.

This pattern which was established from the beginning was continued. Sacrifices were given as a temporary means of acting out the truth that sin must be paid for. It was God's unfailing love that made this possible and his justice which made it necessary.

The cross was God's great love gesture to the world; it was God saying "I love you" to the world. The judgment of Holy God demanded the cross and the love of an all-gracious God permitted it. In mercy God withholds the condemnation we deserve. In grace God gives the forgiveness and restoration we do not deserve.

The cross is God's supreme effort to provide for the forgiveness of mankind. It was on the cross that God's greatest self-disclosure takes place. His own sacrifice through cruel agony and death was enough to give validity to all sacrifices of the past and enough to provide salvation for all generations of the future.

Every aspect of God's nature has a part in the atonement. God reveals Himself as Father, Son and Holy Spirit. The Father is all majesty and power. He is all love and justice. He is all mercy and grace. He is all forgiveness and wrath. In the cross he reveals his very nature in each of these attributes. We cannot and should not seek to separate one of these aspects of God's nature from the other. It is God's holy love and judgment that caused him to come in human form into the world. Jesus said, "He who has seen me has seen the Father" (John 14:9) and Paul declares "For in him the whole fulness of deity dwells bodily" (Col. 2:9). The Son of God is the human expression of God—the God-man. The Father has set forth the Son as a means of expiation and forgiveness. Christ manifested the love of God and the judgment of God upon sin in his life of radical obedience. This obedience found its most complete expression in the cross. In the humanness of Jesus all the human family finds a point of identification.

THE LAMB OF GOD

The name "Lamb of God" was applied twice to Jesus by John the Baptist following his baptism—once in John 1:29 and again in John 1:36. The use of the name "Lamb of God" conveyed the idea of persecuted innocence, and thus the idea of deliverance at the Passover. A widely-used symbol of victory in early Christian art was the lamb carrying the cross.

The letter to the Hebrews represents the most elaborate attempt in the New Testament to interpret the cross in terms of the sacrificial system.[6] To understand this relationship we must keep in mind the pattern of the ritual of sacrifices, particularly that of the "Day of Atonement." It is made clear in Hebrews that what the temple sacrifices could not do, Christ could do and actually had done. To Paul, the law was only "a shadow of good things to come" (Heb. 10:1). It is this contrast between the Old Testament lamb of sacrifice and our Lord Jesus Christ, the eternal Lamb, that we shall pursue here.

Within the subject of "the Lamb" is carried the complete story of God's plan for man as seen through the perspective of the God-man. We can see how necessary this is for us, for man's knowledge of himself and his purpose will never be complete aside from the role of the redeemer sacrifice.

How strange are God's ways. "For the heavens are higher than the earth, so are my ways higher than your ways" (Isa. 55:9). Who would choose a lamb as a symbol and example? Man wants to resemble the lion or the bear. Only God would select the lamb as the animal of sacrifice and give Christ the role of the Lamb to accomplish the mightiest work of the universe and of eternity.

Here is an animal very familiar to us, but so strangely different from all others. The lamb has no defenses. It cannot fly, climb or fight its foes. It has no fangs or claws to resist attack. In fact, the lamb can hardly run and is certainly a prey to insects and beasts; no friends of the sheep can be found. The lamb usually approaches danger and death silent, as if it had been denied by nature the bare solace of a cry. Yet, all these are a part of God's reason for using the lamb as a symbol of divine sacrifice.

God's Lamb is a picture of holiness as one "without blemish" (1 Pet. 1:19). This is an important quality which is evident from a close study of Leviticus. The work that the Lamb of sacrifice performed on the cross required absolute holiness. No blemish was found in him or in the finished product of his plan.

The aspect of complete dependence is another integral part of the nature of God's Lamb. "The Son can do nothing of his own accord," said Jesus (John 5:19). This is stating simply that the Father must be active in and through the Son, our Savior. Embodied in the Lamb is the very nature and essence of God himself. Just as the branch is dependent upon the vine, so the Lamb is dependent upon God.

This is another necessary and natural characteristic of God's Lamb—complete helplessness. The Lamb must be defenseless in order to demonstrate the triumphs of the weak. Christ won by losing. He was victorious by defeat. His death was the only way to procure life.

God's way is so mysterious to the natural man and to the carnal mind. Only as we see the Lamb of God as victorious can we explain the victory songs of millions of martyrs. They, too, won by their death. They conquered by surrendering. They overcame evil with good. This very idea is at the heart of Christ's philosophy. The command "resist not evil" was the tactic which led him to the cross and in that one event made him eternal victor.

THE PASSOVER LAMB

Christ meets the requirements of the Passover lamb in every detail. There must have been this same conviction in the mind of the Apostle Paul, who said, "For Christ, our paschal lamb, has been sacrificed for us" (1 Cor. 5:7). The description of the Passover is found in the twelfth chapter of Exodus. First, the passover lamb was kept in isolation from the tenth to the fourteenth of the month (Nisan) (Exod. 12:3–7). In compliance with this our Lord was kept in prison through the night preceding his trial (Luke 22:54). When he was arrested, Jesus said to those who took him, "Day after day I was with you in the temple teaching, and you did not seize me. But let the scriptures be fulfilled" (Mark 14:49).

The Passover lamb must also be a male lamb without blemish (Exod. 12:5). Christ is the price of our redemption and he is called the "lamb without blemish or spot" (1 Pet. 1:19). This is the very reason Christ's bones were not broken as were those of the thieves who died on each side of him. He remained the unblemished Lamb until his last breath. It was a part of the mechanism of crucifixion to break the legs of the victim. This breaking of the legs would throw the entire weight of the body upon the arms, intensify the pain and thereby hasten death. Yet Jesus' legs were not broken like those of the thieves.

While this was a part of God's plan, we cannot help but notice how much our Lord suffered in our behalf. Physicians will affirm that the weight of the body against the arms fixes the rib cage and thus respiration can take place only in diaphragmatic action. After a prolonged period of suspension, the diaphragm will become fatigued and finally complete paralysis of the stomach muscles will occur. The fastening of the legs and feet enables the victim to relieve this respiratory failure by providing a point of leverage to raise the body and thus alleviate the tension on the throat set up by the body weight hanging on the arms. This prolongs the agony of crucifixion and victims may continue to surge and plunge in this way for several hours.

When the legs are broken, the point of leverage is removed and the victim dies of respiratory failure. Thus, the breaking of the legs is to be understood as an act of mercy, not as an act of torture. It was to hasten the death of the crucified. The leg-breaking took place at the end of the process of execution. Yet Jesus was already dead and there was no need for his legs to be broken. One of the soldiers, however, wanted to make sure that Jesus had not simply lapsed into a coma, "pierced his side with a spear" (John 19:34). The physical effects of crucifixion bear out the events of the sacrifices of Jesus as presented in the Gospels.

Blood played an important part in the Passover sacrifice. It is the blood on the altar that makes an atonement for the soul. (Lev. 17:11). It is the blood on the doorposts that makes the passover. (Exod. 12:7b). However, salvation "from" something is not enough. Back of the thought of atonement and sacrifice we see the first reason, God's ultimate motive— love and joy. God will have his people to his heart in spite of sin and separation.

God's altars sanctify all gifts that pass between himself and his children. Little did we think that the very gibbet to which the Lamb of God was nailed would become an altar. Nothing of this blessed fact ever entered the minds of our Lord's crucifiers. But when they made him a place to die, they also made a blessed meeting place between God and his people. It was the blood of their sacrifice that marked the way to God and none marked it more clearly than the "blood of his cross" (Col. 1:20).

SUMMARY

Nowhere in physical or spiritual geography can one see so far and view so much as from the hill called "Calvary." All the ages focus on that point of time which Christ called "my hour" (John 2:4). His blood and his sacrifice connect with eternity. This one event in history unites forever an estranged heaven and earth, a fallen humanity and a holy God.

There is a golden cord of divine purpose running from the cross into eternity. Therefore, we cannot look at the cross as an accident. It was a predetermined act of God. Those who crucified him did in their ignorance what God had "predestined to take place" (Acts 4:28). Before his death Jesus set the scene by saying "I have earnestly desired to eat this passover with you before I suffer" (Luke 22:15).

Christ is identified with our death to sin and self. He is the one redeeming member of a fallen race. He was the only one whose nature and essence made him a suitable sacrifice. Being the only "Holy One" of the human family, he was destined to die "to sin, once for all" (Rom. 6:10). Only in his perfect nature and divine sacrifice can atonement be made.

V

THE CROSS AND
MAN

The hands of Christ
Seem very frail,
For they were broken
By a nail.

But only they reach
Heaven at last
Whom these frail, broken
Hands hold fast.
        John Richard
        Moreland

Father, forgive them; for they know not what they do (Luke 23:34).

Mankind is overwhelmed by the meaningless evil
of life. He seeks to find in religion the meaning of
life. He seeks salvation from suffering, basic evil, sin
and death. The cross of Jesus Christ stands as the
answer for the dilemma in which man finds himself.
The salvation offered through the cross of Christ deals
with the whole man, "the moral self set in a physical
body, intimately related to that self." [1] When man
turns through faith to the cross, salvation is experienced as a reality. The complexities of life find perspective. When man turns through faith to the cross
he acknowledges the place of Christ in his life. The
cross becomes a symbol of self-denial, a symbol of
eternal and abundant life.

SYMBOL OF SELF-DENIAL

Having experienced and expressed self-effacement
all through his earthly life and ministry, Christ knew
the challenge of self-denial. The supreme test of self-
giving was before him as he spoke to his disciples about
self-denial. The passage found in Mark 8:34–38 was
spoken by our Lord only a few months before he endured the pain and death of the cross. No doubt he
knew what was ahead for him as he spoke to them of
losing their lives for his sake and for the gospel's.

Real men always respond favorably to a great challenge of enduring hardships. Christ never deceived anyone about what was involved in following him. He
does not deceive us today. He offers us a cross of self-
denial and self-sacrifice. His ethic teaches us to put
him first, others next and ourselves last—always in
that order. His cross was one of self-giving and self-
denial. The cross he gives to us must also be one upon
which self is put to death.

Christ gave a call to self-denial. He would never

ask us to do what he himself was unwilling to do. He has set the example for us. Just as Christ *chose* the cross, so must we choose it. A cross is never forced upon us when we are unwilling to bear it. The challenge is given. We hear the Master call, "Take up your cross daily and follow me." To do this requires saying "No" to self and "Yes" to Christ. It requires giving up self-preferment, ease and comfort. God must come first. This is what is meant by the idea of "death to self."

Here is exposed the very heart of the Christian secret of a happy life. Paul had discovered this secret when he so courageously said, "I have been crucified with Christ; it is no longer I who live, but Christ who lives in me" (Gal. 2:20). When one is *crucified,* his whole self is put to death. Paul meant that he had been put to death as far as his selfish and sinful nature were concerned. When he died to self, he became alive in Christ—not in his own power, but because Christ came to live fully within him. So it is with every follower of Christ who takes up the cross of self-denial.

Jesus taught that when one becomes his disciple, he must put others ahead of himself and God ahead of others. This is not easy. The very idea is contrary to the natural urges of life. Yet it is possible with the help of God's Holy Spirit who indwells the Christian's life. We face this decision every day and it is never easy to choose self-denial. Taking up our crosses then means that we choose to put self in a subordinate position to others and to God. This calls for constant effort and daily surrender to Christ.

SYMBOL OF ETERNAL LIFE

Our Lord's words had a literal meaning for many Christians of the first century. His followers were to understand that if they gave up their lives in this

world, they would gain life *eternal* after death. To lose
their lives was in reality to gain life. This truth still applies to us whether or not we face the threat of physical
death.

In our land today we are preoccupied with pre-
serving life. There is a frenzied search for products
and practices that will aid us in our attempt to *save*
our lives. If we save life for ourselves it will be lost
to God. Yet if we lose life for God it will come back
to us as life at its best. Those who have forgotten their
own selfish concerns and have spent themselves for
others have found the real meaning in life. Jesus established the everlasting and practical principle of
self-denial. The old man of sin and unbelief dies at
conversion. The new man of faith and commitment is
born. Immersion symbolizes this experience. According to Paul, by baptism "we were buried therefore
with him into death, so that as Christ was raised from
the dead by the glory of the Father, we too might walk
in newness of life" (Rom. 6:4).

For a Christian this death is more traumatic than
physical death. It is death to sin—the death of a self-
willed person. New and eternal life begins out of this
death; we are resurrected into a new life. For such a
believer there will be no interruption when the body
dies. Physical death for a Christian will simply be like
walking through a doorway into a greater realization
of the life already begun in him. This is what Jesus
meant when he told Martha, "Whoever lives and believes in me shall never die" (John 11:26). On the
cross Jesus gave us the hope of eternal life. The symbol of the cross still speaks his message and reminds
us of our task.

SYMBOL OF ABUNDANT LIFE

Emil Brunner has said that modern man, who, for

the sake of his freedom, emancipated himself from God and became godless, is the destroyer of himself.[2] Without Christ man cannot know the secret of the abundant life.

We usually accept the idea of eternal life without asking when it begins. According to the Word of God, our eternal life begins the moment we accept God's gift of salvation. Through repentance and confession of sin and casting ourselves upon the forgiving grace of Christ, we are saved. This is salvation from a sinner's life, a sinner's death and a sinner's destiny. We are saved forever, forgiven, received by the Father as a son and heir—all this and heaven, too. This is life that will never end. How good to be able to enjoy eternal life in the here and now.

Life after life will be easy, we say, but how can we live like it now? As long as we are in the flesh, we are tempted and tried. We are always confronted by the world, the flesh and the devil.

The cross is symbolic to the Christian way of life as well as death. Because we live in the world, we have to live in the midst of sin. We share the horror of war, the struggle for survival, the suffering of disease and the hurt of wrongdoing. As long as we are a part of the world, we must, of necessity, share its sufferings. Because we are alive in Christ with new life, we could not be satisfied just to sit by and keep our hands clean while others suffer so much. Thus, we are moved to become carriers of God's blessings to others. We become bearers of his light to those who are caught up in darkness. We seek to *live* within two different worlds—this world and the Kingdom of God. Our task demands that we be good citizens of each of these kingdoms. Life after life is just a continuation of life in Christ which we live first here on this earth. We seek to demonstrate to our fellowman that life in

Christ can be victorious and that it is the only life worth living twice—here and hereafter.

SUMMARY

Ministry is the way of the cross. In the cross is the supreme example of one giving himself for others. The cross is truly a symbol of self-denial. We can never remove the idea of compassion and service from our concept of the believer's cross. Ours is the privilege and responsibility of ministry because of the cross. Our response to Jesus and his sacrifice means that we can no longer live our lives by instinctive desires. We can no longer love the things our natures tell us to adore. But, rather than just giving mental acceptance to these ideals we must go on to embody them and express them. Being a Christian, then, is letting Jesus Christ walk into the world in our bodies. It is no longer our own goodness, but the goodness of Jesus that is seen in us. When Christ lives in us we know the secret of the abundant life and look forward to eternal life in him.

The cross calls to us to *come,* but it also sends us out with a vision of the crucified burning in our hearts. We have a message that must be carried into the world. The cross compels us to *go* and minister lovingly in the name of Christ. This is what it means to take up a cross. Making choices in the light of eternity, we can enthrone the living Christ in our hearts. Then he who opened to us the way of salvation shall open the gates to his Kingdom and say "Come, O blessed of my Father, inherit the Kingdom prepared for you" (Matt. 25:34).

Part 3

THE BELIEFS ABOUT

THE CROSS

VI

THE CROSS AND
FAITH

E'er since by faith I saw the stream
Thy flowing wounds supply,
Redeeming love has been my theme,
And shall be till I die.
      William Cowper
      "There Is a Fountain"

Hear, O Israel: The Lord our God is one Lord;
and you shall love the Lord your God with all
your heart, and with all your soul, and with all
your might. And these words which I command
you this day shall be upon your heart (Deut.
6:4–5).

For I am not ashamed of the gospel: it is the
power of God for salvation to every one who has
faith. . . . For in it the righteousness of God
is revealed through faith for faith; as it is written,
"He who through faith is righteous shall live!"
(Rom. 1:16–17).

Martin Luther was one of the greatest religious leaders of history. He did more than any other man to establish what we call the Protestant tradition. Luther read the New Testament in the light of Paul's statement that "the just shall live by faith" (Rom. 1:17 KJV). This truth became the central idea of the reformation. Faith is a living, restless thing. It cannot be inoperative. We are not saved by works, but if there are no works, there must be something amiss with faith.

No doubt this was a great revelation to Luther. Faith, as the only way to God, was a new idea to the medieval church. Yet, no one can deny the influence Luther brought upon the church of his day because he held this truth up before his peers.

It is at this very point we must consider the centrality of faith in God's redemptive work on the cross. Through faith in Christ we have access to God and to eternal life. The meaning and nature of true faith is essential to understanding the cross.

God's eternal purpose is the salvation of sinners. This is the only possible solution to the mystery of the incarnation, crucifixion and resurrection. Faith in Christ is the only condition through which man can come to possess this salvation. Christ has brought God's gift to perishing man, yet only by faith can the gift be possessed. The only proper response of man to God's atoning work is faith. John's gospel is an adequate summary of this truth. He affirms that salvation is by faith and faith only. John never uses the noun form of the word *faith,* but he uses the verb form time and time again. Paul speaks as a theologian and contends that by faith, and by faith alone, men are to be justified.[1]

THE MEANING OF FAITH

In John's gospel the term *faith* is used as a refer-

ence to those who "believe on his name" those who
have "received" Christ. John also speaks of those who
have "come to the light." It is also a figure of faith
that finds expression in the statements of Jesus in
which he speaks of "drinking his blood" and "eating
the flesh" of the Son of man. John's word means more
than our word "believe." We can see the meaning of
this term more clearly if we keep in mind that at the
heart of faith is the idea of trust and committal as an
act of the will. Faith means far more than acceptance
of an idea with the intellect on the basis of evidence.
The Christian use of the word *faith,* as it is expressed
in the entire New Testament, carries the meaning of
being made right with God through Jesus Christ. It is
exactly the same in the Old Testament. *Faith* is always
the way to be made right with God. Brunner said that
this faith must involve "the surrender of one's own
person and its claims, its self-will, in favor of the living God who confronts it in Christ. Faith is the utmost
conceivable personal deed, a self-surrender to the self-
offering Redeemer. Faith in Jesus Christ implies a
total transformation of one's personal existence." [2]

Faith, says John, is normally a growing thing. In
most instances of dramatic conversion in the New Testament, we can feel the growth and development of
the individual's faith. For instance, in John 1, we see
five men who came in contact with Jesus and became
his disciples. First, they accepted the idea that he is
the Messiah. But in chapter 2 they witnessed the first
miracle of Jesus, and John says "they believed on
Him." Of course, they believed on him before, but
after they saw his power, their faith became clearer
and more definite. Here faith is shown to be a growing
and enriching experience. Full-fledged faith is trust in
God which brings eternal life and which makes the believer a child of God. It brings him into union with

the Father and with the Son. This is in full agreement with Paul's idea of faith. Paul sees faith as the quality of trust and total commitment which brings the believer into a right relationship with God. Just as faith is the quality which makes salvation possible, it is faith which keeps and sustains the believer.

Faith is in the highest sense an act of self-determination whereby one definitely surrenders himself to God. It is the act of receiving God's grace of God. Now to go a step further, faith is the quality of soul which makes a child of God want to be like the Savior. A state of fellowship with Christ is the result of faith. To believe in Christ is to have fellowship with him. Genuine faith continues as a permanent state of character. Jesus said, "If you continue in my word, you are truly my disciples" (John 8:31).

Looking back to Abraham we can see this genuine faith expressed. "And he believed the Lord and he reckoned it to him as righteousness" (Gen. 15:6). This same quality must be present before any sacrifice can be meaningful. Without faith it is impossible to please God. This has always been the case between man and God. It is true today. The Saviour calls all men to believe in him and then keep on believing in him until faith becomes sight.

THE EXPRESSION OF FAITH

True faith will find expression either in deed, word or thought. Genuine faith cannot be hidden. The expression is actually a part of the very nature of faith. Faith that is not expressed is like a bird without wings, like a boat that cannot float, like a lamp that gives no light. This kind of faith cannot exist because when it can't find expression it ceases to be faith at all. It is a self-contradiction.

The verb form of the word faith is an *action* word. "To faith" God is to trust him, to cast one's self on his mercy and grace. Thus, one cannot really believe in God without casting himself upon him completely. By expressing our faith we respond to God with all that is in us. Because we believe God is good, we can live in the security that such faith offers. The life of a Christian is good, but it is not always pleasant or easy. Being in Christ complicates our thinking, speaking, and living. Yet our security is in the will of God.

These are times that demand a strong and productive faith—saving faith. As Paul said to the jailer in Philippi, "Believe in the Lord Jesus, and you will be saved, you and your household" (Acts 16:31). A belief that saves must begin with God, the sovereign creator. Here is the beginning point—to believe that God does exist and that he alone has brought everything into existence. Hear the Apostle Paul again as he states, "And without faith it is impossible to please him for whoever would draw near to God must believe that He exists and that He rewards those who seek him" (Heb. 11:6). But to believe that God does exist is not enough to save a single soul. It was this very point to which the Spirit spoke through James saying, "You believe that God is one; you do well. Even the demons believe—and shudder" (James 2:19). Let no man say that he is a Christian on the basis of belief that there is a God. Christianity involves more than an acceptance of God—much more.

The next step in faith is to believe that Jesus Christ is God in the flesh. He who was a real person, a unique combination of God and man. This great truth is emphasized clearly by Dr. E. Y. Mullins, who points out that Jesus disclosed the very inner being of God because he *is* God.[3] So then, to accept the New Testament account of Christ is to believe in a Christ who is Lord and Messiah. The idea of the deity of Jesus is summarized by the Apostle Peter, who said, "God has made him both Lord and Christ, this Jesus whom you crucified" (Acts 2:36). Step two in faith is to believe that Jesus was fully God and fully man, the God-man. Dr. Truett was right when he said of that word, "Never did a hyphen mean so much." But to believe that Jesus was God is not enough to save you.

The third step in faith is to believe that when Jesus died on the cross he died for you personally as if you were the only person on earth to be died for. His death was the purchase price of salvation for every individual on earth. He died for me and for you in a uniquely personal death. Brunner, in his book *Eternal Hope,* says, "The historical event on Calvary, fundamentally appreciable by everyone as such, is the visible shell of the invisible kernel—the absolutely unique—which can only be apprehended by faith.[4]

No other could have paid the price of our redemption. Jesus became our sacrifice and died in our place. If we can believe in a God who is alive and present, then we can believe that he, through Jesus Christ, bore our sins in his own body on the cross. As shocking and as strange as it might sound, this is not enough to save us. All these aspects of belief are essential, but not completely sufficient for salvation. The final step is to believe all these truths enough to completely yield and surrender the heart and life to Christ. When a man believes the gospel enough to lay his life in God's hands, to allow God to break his will and forgive him of his sin—that is a faith which saves. It is a faith of saving quality for it embraces the very truth of the gospel. It is a faith of quality because it is sincere and deep enough to bring about a transformation of the life and the inner man.

The nature of faith has not changed since the beginning of time. The physical symbols of God's redemptive purpose have changed, but the saving response has remained the same. That response is *faith*. The rituals, the sacrifices and the symbols of the Old Testament all fade away in the light of Christ's cross. The brilliance of the cross outshines all the altars of the ancients and dominates the scene of all God's redemptive activity. While these outward symbols of God's saving grace have changed with man's ability to grasp them, the single factor of faith has, of necessity, been present whenever forgiveness and redemption were realized. There can never be forgiveness without faith. There can never be growth in God's grace without faith. Our witness to God's power and presence depends upon it. Faith is the key to man's relationship to God—in every age, in every place.

THE EXPERIENCE OF FAITH

Faith is experienced as man responds to the saving work of God as seen in the cross of Jesus Christ. In the light of the cross man sees himself as an unworthy sinner. The cross calls to man to leave his sin—to repent of his sin—and to turn his total life over to God.

Faith means accepting the forgiveness of God as a free gift. Christ has purchased that forgiveness. It is accepted only as a gift. It cannot be earned, nor can it ever be deserved. God never allows man to consider his forgiveness as a thing to be merited. He gives eternal life to all who believe in him and accept his salvation. The cross of Jesus is the signature of God that certifies that the sinner's debt is paid in full.

Faith means that a person receives Christ as his deliverer. When man sees in Jesus the only means of his deliverance, he is accepting God's provision for his everlasting life. Christ says "Behold, I stand at the door and knock; if any one hears my voice and opens the door, I will come in to him and eat with him, and he with me" (Rev. 3:20). He is the waiting guest at the door of every sinner's heart. To accept him as the deliverer and Savior is the experience of faith.

THE FINALITY OF FAITH

Faith means trusting Christ with one's eternal destiny. Intellectual assent to the fact of the cross is not enough. Real faith is to put one's life for time and eternity in God's hands because of what Christ has done for us. In the fullness of faith a man must come to the point of casting himself completely and finally on the mercy of a loving Savior. Then he can say with the writer of the hymn:

> Nothing in my hand I bring,
> Simply to Thy cross I cling;
> Naked, come to Thee for dress,
> Helpless, look to Thee for grace;
> Foul, I to the fountain fly,
> Wash me Saviour, or I die.[5]

Christ is the final sacrifice of God for the sins of mankind. Yet that is not all that must be said. The death of Jesus *saves* only those who respond to it. Conversion means action; a man must take a definite stand—a personal stand.

From the cross the dying Savior cried, "It is finished" (John 19:30). No more final statement could be made. The Mediator had thus completed the work of redemption. He had opened the door to heaven. He had defeated all the enemies of the soul. It was his final cry of victory over sin, death and the grave. Christ made the final declaration of God's grace. In him all the fulness of God's purpose reaches its culmination. "There is one God, and there is one mediator between God and men, the man Christ Jesus" (1 Tim. 2:5). Jesus said, "I am the way" (John 14:6). Thus, he alone can forgive sin, save the soul or bestow the gift of eternal life.

The fact of faith is fundamental. This one response is the only one God requires and the only one he will accept. By faith mankind can experience the new birth. By faith mankind can bear fruit of regeneration. By faith old things pass away and all things become new. By faith in Christ we pass from death unto life.

The cross offers God's guarantee that we can share the life he offers so freely, and we can sing with never-failing confidence:

> Uplifted are the gates of brass;
> The bars of iron yield;
> Behold the King of glory pass!
> The cross hath won the field!

VII

THE CROSS AND SACRIFICE

The atonement is not the cause of God's love,
But Love is the cause of the atonement.
                                        Charles Hall

Be silent before the Lord God!
  For the day of the Lord is at hand;
the Lord has prepared a sacrifice
  and consecrated his guests.
And on the day of the Lord's sacrifice—
"I will punish the officials and the king's sons
And all who array themselves in foreign attire"
(Zeph. 1:7–8).

One major problem in understanding the sacrifices of the Jews is that varying interpretations have been placed upon them from one period of Israel's history to another. At times the people attached more importance to certain sacrifices than others. It is obvious that the practice of sacrifice was a part of the efforts of the worshipper to come before God (Jehovah) in an acceptable fashion. Making a sacrifice represented man's obedience to God's commands. Yet, the sacrifices were a medium of divine communication through which God gave assurance of the forgiveness of sin.

BELIEFS OF THE OLD TESTAMENT

The Jews made the sacrifices so much a part of their nationalistic spirit that they became a symbol of Jewish nationalism. This was a *result* of their ardent devotion to the practice of sacrificing rather than a part of God's plan. The personal aspect of this response underlies all spiritual implications of the sacrifices. This strong nationalistic spirit helped the Jews to gradually slip into the fallacy of thinking the sacrifices could bring God's forgiveness to the nation as a whole. They lost sight of the need for faith and obedience. These rituals constantly reminded the Jews that their God was sovereign and ever-present with them. They kept him central in their practice of sacrifice, for it was his righteousness and holiness that demanded the death of an innocent one. Gradually, over hundreds of years, the Jews came to see in these sacrifices the attitude of Holy God toward sin. They came to understand that God abhors man's sin while he loves the sinner. It was this very understanding that represents a higher level of response to God from the people of Israel. This tells us that their knowledge of God had been increasing through the years. Their quest for forgiveness now has more meaning than before. No longer were the sacrifices made in order to prevent the judgment of God, but to identify with the purity of this offering to God.

The sacrifices had no power to save. There was no automatic atonement in the ritual. The prophets of Israel made this point very clear in their fiery denunciations of sacrifices. They cried out against the idea that God could be bribed by the offerings. Without the attitude of repentance for sin the sacrifices could accomplish nothing. For example, note this verse from Leviticus:

> When a man is guilty in any of these, he shall confess the sin he has committed, and he shall bring his guilt offering to the Lord for his sin which he has committed, . . . and the priest shall make atonement for him for his sin (Lev. 5:5–6).

Being forgiven depended on the attitude of the sinner and on his personal confession of his wrong. The "guilt offering" was merely an expression of that repentance and could in itself never remove the guilt of sin. Furthermore, the law made it mandatory for a sinner or law-breaker to make restitution for his wrong. He was commanded to confess his sin, to repay in kind whatever he had stolen and then add to that an additional twenty percent to show a genuine desire for forgiveness. This is clearly stated in Numbers 5:6.

The function of sacrifice, then, was to be a medium between God and man. In the sacrifices God showed the divine disposition of judgment and mercy. Man performed these sacrifices through faith and obedience. As a part of his performance of the ritual, man was compelled to repent, confess and forsake his sin. Here God established the contact between man's faith and

God's grace. Many eminent scholars of the Old Testament agree that this position gives proper evaluation of the saving significance of the sacrifices. This is God's appointed way for man to express his faith and obedience to the living God. The complete covering and removal of sin are included in this understanding of the sacrifices. In this sense the sacrifices are only the *means* of forgiveness, not salvation in or of itself.[1]

SACRIFICE AS SEEN FROM THE NEW TESTAMENT PERSPECTIVE

When we look back on the sacrifices through the perspective of the New Testament, we see them as a means to an end, not and end in themselves. These rituals were never intended to impart forgiveness from God. The necessary aspects in obtaining God's forgiveness were: faith in the living God, confession of sin, repentance for sin, and restitution for sin. Without these there could be no forgiveness.

This system of sacrifice parallels the sacrifice of Christ upon the cross in that he took upon himself all the guilt of repentant sinners of all time. He became our substitute and bore our sins in his own body on the cross. The animal sacrifice became the recipient of the sinner's guilt and actually became the recipient of his punishment. As repentance and confession took place in the sinner himself, forgiveness was then received. Thus, the Old Testament Jew was forgiven in the same manner we are forgiven. He came to God through the innocent sacrifice just as we come to God. The true worshipper came in faith, repentance and confession, the same way we come.

God alone can forgive sins. There is no other source of salvation. He has never changed the basic requirements for mankind. All who come to him must come in faith: "Without faith it is impossible to please him. For whoever would draw near to God must believe that he exists and that he rewards those who seek him" (Heb. 11:6). Since we have the same God we have the same basic requirement for salvation. The act of sacrifice will not save unless the "beholder" has faith in the God to whom the sacrifice is made.[2] The death of Christ, our sacrifice, is likewise valid enough to save all those who come to him in faith and repentance.

It is obvious to even the casual reader that the writers of the New Testament make constant use of Old Testament language and thought patterns. This is true to the extent that one can almost feel Judaism and Christianity are actually the same religion. Perhaps this is intended in the New Testament. At any rate, it is true that Jesus is referred to as a sacrifice. Christ is called the "Lamb of God" and "offering of sweet smell."

On the other hand, Jesus himself made no charges that seem to indicate that sacrifices were not valid and effective to those who offered them in true repentance and faith. The religion of Israel was real to the first century Christians, so real in fact that the New Testament writers were able to see the power of an "Eternal Priest" who was a mediator for all time and unto all people. Therefore, the unity of Christianity and Judaism will serve as an adequate basis for raising this question. There are also many things that could be said for this point of view as we look at the nature of salvation in the religion of Israel.

The question of sacrifice itself broadens in scope when we dare examine the logic and deeper meaning of this development. All religious symbols are merely the significant or peculiar use of material objects to represent the divine. In the case of the religion of Israel, the symbol was sacrificial ritual.

THE NATURE OF SACRIFICE

Sacrifice is an outward movement which was used to express man's feeling of devotion and adoration for God whom he worshipped. By definition the same can be said for those many liturgical movements made in our worship today that are significant to expressions of worship. Therefore, we could well agree that a sacrifice to the ancient Jew was merely an outward expression of inward experience. P. T. Forsyth opens new doors of insight for us by his statement to this effect. He is willing to grant that the sacrifices, as a whole, did serve as an outward expression of the inward faith of those sincere worshipers who practiced them.[3]

It has already been pointed out that the ritual could by no means transmit forgiveness of sins, but all that forgiveness must come from God. Again, we come to the fact that if it is God alone who saves, then man is not in a position to state the terms on which the forgiveness will be received. God gives his terms on how the forgiveness will be dispensed. This is to say that God accepts that which he will and, if it is acceptable to God, it must be acceptable to man.[4] The very nature of sacrifice as an expression of man's adoration for God and man's helplessness without God indicates that God alone can give value to the ritual.

Also, the sacrifice when rightly offered was believed to be charged with power. This power is not described, but in every case the power of the sacrificial rite was accredited to God as having been given by him. That the sacrifice was thought to be an organ of the spirit

and not effective within itself is held very firmly by
H. H. Rowley. Rowley also makes much of the fact
that restitution was to be made in every case where
such was possible. The making of adequate restitution
in the spirit of repentance and much remorse for sin
which had been committed was clearly required by
the law (Lev. 1:4, 3:2, 4:4–7).

There is also something to be said for the prophetic
attack on the sacrifices. In many cases very little quali-
fication is made by the prophets as to what type of
sacrifices were included. One would readily ascertain
that all sacrifices were included. However, even if this
were true, there is an understandable reason behind
the condemnatory note in the prophetic strain.

Perhaps explanation can be found in the fact that
the ritual lost most of its real meaning to people. The
people began to perform the required sacrifices without the required inward remorse for sin. The form was
present, but the meaning slowly died. More than likely,
it was a case of the people turning away from the
sacrifices rather than the sacrifices turning from the
people.

The system of sacrifice became inadequate to meet
the needs of the people, but this is not to say the sacrificial system was in itself evil and worthy of all of
the condemnation received from the prophets. In order
to restore the heart to their religion, the prophets re-
sorted to pleading for inward righteousness, not just
a meaningless adherence to the law. It might well be
the case that this could not have been even partially
accomplished without an open and unqualified attack
on the whole system of offering things to God on the
altar. It should also be pointed out that this condemnation was a rather late development in the religion of
Israel and is more prominent in the post-exilic
prophets.

SUMMARY

The value of sacrifice was not only to establish but also to maintain a community of worshipers. This served not only to shorten the great gulf between God and man in the Old Testament, but also to continually draw out of man the highest and best for God. The sacrifice was to the worshiper a common meal which bound the participants, a gift of life which was in some way to invoke the goodness of God upon him and which was a constant reminder of the covenant he had made with God. Though much stock is placed in the forgiveness of sins committed against God and sins committed against man, we can see something of a changing concept of God as holy and just all through the system itself. It is this *nature of sacrifice* that we sought to explain in the light of God's eternal redemption of pre-Christian man. The sacrifices, no matter how complex the system, were greatly valuable in the salvation of every forgiven sinner. They represented man's reaching out for God and God's reaching down for man; in the sacrifices they met and communicated.

God provided an eternal atonement for men. This is the great fact over which we should rejoice. God had from the very beginning seen that man's plight was such that no less than the greatest of all sacrifices could help him. So, in the light of man's need and God's unfailing love for His creatures, the sacrifice was provided. The blood was spilt as before, the altar was a cross of wood, the priest was none other than God himself, and the cost of the sacrifice on the cross was more valuable to God than all other sacrifices offered together. Yet, we must ask ourselves if the world might someday commit the great sin that those Jews did—coming to the altar with no repentance beholding the sacrifice, but only with their eyes.

VIII

THE CROSS AND
SALVATION

Not all the blood of beasts,
On Jewish altars slain,
Could give the guilty conscience peace,
Or wash away the stain.

But Christ, the Heavenly Lamb,
Takes all our sins away;
A sacrifice of nobler name,
And richer blood than they.
      Isaac Watts

For if the sprinkling of defiled persons with the blood of goats and bulls and with the ashes of a heifer sanctifies for the purification of the flesh, how much more shall the blood of Christ, who through the eternal Spirit offered himself without blemish to God, purify your conscience from dead words to serve the living God (Heb. 9:13–14).

The idea of salvation in the Old Testament has produced varied and even conflicting views. Some Biblical scholars believe that Jesus' death could not benefit the Jews who lived before the crucifixion. Others believe that salvation for the "pre-Christian" Jews was possible only because of the promised sacrifice fulfilled in the death of Jesus Christ. The Jews' sacrifices were very closely bound to their worship and sacred rituals.

SALVATION AND SACRIFICE

All of the Jewish sacrifices were expressions of faith and obedience toward God. From the beginning of creation, the cross of Jesus was a fact in the heart and mind of God. John called Christ "the Lamb slain from the foundation of the world" (Rev. 13:8 KJV). Yet, because he had not yet actually died on the cross, God gave instructions for certain sacrifices to be made as an indication of Israel's faith and obedience. God knew that Jesus was going to die physically. Yet this sacrifice was not the medium of salvation for those who lived and died before Jesus was crucified. Let's notice several facts about these Old Testament sacrifices.

First, God commanded the Jews to perform the sacrifices. He described the rituals in great detail and gave specific instructions about each one. They were not man-made rituals. God required a sacrifice that was in keeping with his holiness and righteousness. The idea that the Jews sacrificed animals in disobedience is false because the Bible gives us abundant evidence that God himself initiated the sacrifices.

Second, the sacrifice itself had no power to forgive and cleanse those who offered it. Nothing in the Old Testament leads us to believe that the sacrifices had any redeeming quality at all. Much to the contrary, it was God who forgave the sins of the Jews who made sacrifices. Without exception, the prophets rejected the idea of salvation coming through the sacrifice itself. Only God can forgive sin, and he does so on the basis of faith and obedience. The sacrifices were only evidences of faith and expressions of obedience on the part of repentant people.

Third, notice that the sacrifices were not permanent, but were given to meet a temporary need. The Jews were not ready to accept the idea of *God* suffering and dying for their sins. They did, however, understand that God required the death of a *sinless* one and the shedding of innocent blood. This reminds us of the perfect Lamb of God who was slain for us. We also think of the suffering Savior with the shedding of his blood on the cross in our behalf. Yet the Jews could not think of Jesus when they performed a blood sacrifice. Only when they were ready to receive the eternal Lamb was Jesus to die. God was waiting for the proper time for this sacrifice to be performed. Until that day arrived the sacrifice of animals would be practiced by the faithful and obedient Jews.

Finally, the death of Jesus fits perfectly into the pattern of sacrifices which God gave the Jews. Just as the sacrifice of a goat or lamb could not save without the faith of the sinner, so the sacrifice of the Lamb of God could not save without the faith of the believer. If the *sacrifice* could save, there would be no need for repentance, confession and faith. Some Christians believe that all men who ever lived are saved because Christ died for all mankind. Indeed, he died for all. Yet none can be saved who refuse to believe in him and confess him as Savior and Lord. Salvation is provided for everyone, but it is given only to the repentant sinners who yield to Christ's Lordship and receive his forgiveness.

FAITH AND SACRIFICE

God always deals with his people on the basis of their own understanding of him. He requires faith of all who come to him. Paul states this in the following verse: "And without faith it is impossible to please him; for whoever would draw near to God must believe that he exists and that he rewards those who seek him" (Heb. 11:6).

Faith is the response which God requires of all whom he saves. No one can come to God without believing that he does exist and that he will save those who seek him. It was faith that made salvation possible for the Old Testament Jews. Thus, the requirement for salvation has not changed, only the form of the sacrifice. Faith was the key to salvation and forgiveness before the cross, and it has been since the foundation of the world. Animal sacrifices were offered in obedience to God, but they were mere shadows of the real and lasting sacrifice of Jesus on the cross. Faith, then and now, is necessary to conduct man into a right relationship with God.

The sacrifices gave the Jews of the Old Testament a means of responding to and obeying God. It was that faith which God called forth from them. Their *faith*— not the blood of animal sacrifices—pleased God. The only redeeming feature of the sacrifices was the belief in a forgiving God which was held by those who performed them. The ritual itself could not save, nor could the dead animal on the altar. God required faith in himself then and now as the medium of forgiveness and redemption.

FORM AND FUNCTION

The rituals of sacrifice had many meanings to the

Jews. The idea of a "gift to God" is present in almost
all Hebrew sacrifices. By "gift" or "offering" we mean
the taking of a life in order to release it or to give it
up to God.[1] Thus, the emphasis of the sacrifices was
not on killing, but on setting a life free, thus giving
it to God. This is also the meaning of the blood sacrifices. For sake of comparison, let us recall the words
of our dying Savior who cried, "Father, into Thy
hands I commit my spirit" (Luke 23:46). The re-
leasing of a life to God was always present in sacrifices
which the Jews made.

Many of the sacrifices of ancient times were of food
and drink. This perhaps was an evidence of the primitive belief that God, like man, needed nourishment.
Only after many centuries did the Jews come to understand that God is universal spirit who does not have
man's weaknesses and limitations. The practice of offering food and drink is one of the earliest known
forms of sacrifice. The motives behind these various
"gift" sacrifices might have been to win the favor of
God, thus to invoke his blessings and avert his wrath.
As we can see, these are wrong motives which later
made the sacrifices meaningless. The Hebrew word for
sacrifice which is used most often in the Old Testament
means "gift offering." This word is used two hundred
eighty-six times. Another word which means "communion offering" is used only one hundred and twenty-
six times in the Old Testament. This kind of gift and
communion offerings recognized reverence for the majesty of God and faith from within the donor.

The greatest benefit here is to the one who makes
the offering. This is one of the most important aspects
of offerings made for sins. Such gift sacrifices were a
necessary part of the total ritual system of the Hebrews. Most of the sacrifices were either to express
repentance for sins or to celebrate the forgiveness of

God. All sin hurts God, for sin is a violation of his will and a reproach against his sovereign holiness. It is fitting that the sacrifices be directed toward making reconciliation with God. The idea of forgiveness and expiation for sin are interwoven into the sacrifices. These sacrifices were initiated by God; so was the sacrifice of Jesus on the cross. These were an expression of God's love and grace; so was the cross. These were to symbolize the forgiveness and salvation of God; so was the cross. These sacrifices were a symbol of judgment on all sin and sinners who will not recognize them; so was the cross of Jesus.

There is a definite connection in both secular history and the Old Testament between forgiveness and gifts. H. H. Rowley points out that the idea of forgiveness of sins is present in all sacrifices of the Jews except for the thank offering. All these offerings of blood were in some way connected to man's inadequacy and imperfection before God. The making of sacrifices throughout the history of Israel indicates a desire to obey God and receive his forgiveness.[2]

The development of the "sin offering" shows this attempt to secure forgiveness even more than others. This specific offering was designed to deal directly with sins committed in ignorance. Sins committed with a "high hand" were punished by death, according to the law (Num. 15:30). H. Wheeler Robinson says that there were no sacrifices which were specifically designed to deal with sin that was deliberately and voluntarily committed, although the trespass offering seems to come closest to meeting the needs of the willful and voluntary sinner who sought forgiveness.[3]

The primitive forms of sacrifice had very little to do with sin. But, as the religion of Israel grew toward a higher concept of God, the idea of genuine repentance become more prominent in the sacrifices. A greater awareness of moral transgression was the direct result of a growing concept of God. This strengthens the idea that God was not known as fully by the Old Testament Jews as he was when the perfect Lamb of sacrifice died on the cross. It is very important that as God became better known the concepts of sin and forgiveness also became more clearly understood.

IDEA OF SUBSTITUTION

Closely related to the idea of forgiveness of sin is the idea of the sacrifice as a substitute for the worshipper. The ceremonies which require the laying on of hands upon the head of the slain animal were never meant to signify the transmission of sin, although some might think the ceremony was to allow the sins of the guilty sinner to flow into the sacrifice. There *was* an aspect of identification between the sinner and the sacrifice. Keep in mind that the Jews felt as if the sacrifice was being offered up to God and that, in a sense, the worshiper too was being offered. This had nothing to do with the so-called "transfer" of sin from man to an animal. The observance of the "Day of Atonement" was closely connected with this idea of substitution. As in the case of the "scapegoat," the animal was not slain but was chased out into the wilderness to die alone. This symbolized the removal of sin. It was, in fact, the only sacrifice which even gives a hint of dealing with the transmission of sins from the sinner to the animal.

As we view the sacrifices from this point in history, we can see the similarity between these rituals and the atoning death of our Savior on the cross. This concept of sacrifice must be clearly understood in order to see God's redemptive purpose unfolding and reaching its zenith in the cross of Jesus.

Part 4

THE PROCLAMATION OF
THE CROSS

IX

THE CROSS IN
THE TEACHINGS OF PAUL

*I know not how that Calvary's cross
a world from sin could free;
I only know its matchless love
Has brought God's love to me.*
        Harry Webb
        Farrington

But we preach Christ crucified, a stumbling block to Jews and folly to Gentiles (1 Cor. 1:23).

For I decided to know nothing among you except Jesus Christ and Him crucified (1 Cor. 2:2).

Paul was the first and greatest theologian of the Christian church. The "good news" of the crucifixion and resurrection had to be taken outside the framework of Judaism and proclaimed to the whole world. It was Paul who led the way in Christian mission. For Paul the gospel was *the* way of life, not just a way of living and thinking. Paul had spent long years searching in disillusionment, desperation and despair. Suddenly and dramatically, God had turned his life completely around on the road to Damascus. Thus, the crucified and risen Lord became his true master. The gospel burned in his bones, and like Jeremiah he could not keep silent. No one knew better than Paul that when a man is drowning he needs not a lecture on water safety but a Savior.

This is what Paul found in Christianity. Therefore, the message of Paul is void of philosophical speculation and pious jargon. He sees the gospel as a person— Jesus Christ the Lord. Time after time Paul states that he is preaching only "Christ and him crucified." It was not with one sudden blinding flash of light that the Christian gospel came to Paul. It took years of preparation. From his early childhood the hand of God was on him. Saul was a Jew by birth and he remained proud of his heritage and birthright until the end of his life. He was not only a Jew, but a Roman citizen. Frequently he called on his citizenship to get him out of a tight spot. In Philippians he tells of his Jewish heritage:

> "Circumcised the eighth day, of the people of Israel, of the tribe of Benjamin, a Hebrew born of Hebrews; as to the law a Pharisee, as to zeal a persecutor of the church, as to righteousness under the law blameless. But whatever gain I had, I counted as loss for the sake of Christ" (Phil. 3:5–7).

101

This was Saul of Tarsus—devout, determined, and grateful for his Jewish heritage. He was a man of two worlds—Jewish and Greek. God obviously had prepared him as a chosen vessel to carry the gospel outside the narrow confines of Palestine. He is the messenger who was given the unique task of proclaiming and interpreting the Christ-event to Jew and Gentile alike. There have been many interpretations of Paul's Damascus road experience. Yet, from that encounter with the risen Christ, the course of his entire life was changed.

No dream, no fantasy, no result of neurosis could ever have brought about such a dramatic and permanent change in Paul. So real and vital was that experience that he staked his future on it. "I have seen the Lord" was Paul's explanation. It was that simple and that profound. It was the validation of a new faith for Paul. From that moment on, Jesus Christ was the center of his life, the core of his being. To spread the news of Jesus was the ruling passion of his life. "For I would have you to know, brethren, that the gospel which was preached by me is not man's gospel. For I did not receive it from man, nor was I taught it, but it came through a revelation of Jesus Christ" (Gal. 1:11–12).

Paul had not been able to see the truth until he had seen the Lord. Then, after Damascus, he went to Arabia where he "conferred not with flesh and blood." He went away to be alone with God to discover himself and to receive his new direction with his newfound faith.

How did Paul interpret the fact of the crucifixion? There is no doubt that he saw the death of Jesus as God's chosen way of mediating forgiveness to sinners on the sole condition of faith. "As in Adam all die, so also in Christ shall all be made alive" (1 Cor. 15:22). Or again, "For our sake he made him to be sin who knew no sin, so that in him we might become the righteousness of God" (2 Cor. 5:21). Paul sees the cross as God's act in behalf of the fallen human family. This act alone provides a way for fallen man to be reconciled to God. The atonement is in essence the divine reaction of a just God to the sin of the world. To participate in the covenant of forgiveness and salvation requires only a faith response to the crucified and risen Savior. In other words, Christ Jesus atoned for the sins of the whole world by dying on behalf of and in place of man. He took the punishment and death which rightfully belongs to sinners so the sinners could have freedom and life.

DELIVERANCE

The key word to understanding how Paul saw the atonement is *deliverance*. By a faith response to Christ's saving act on the cross, man is delivered out of bondage to sin, self and Satan. This is not our doing. This is the "good news" of Christ's battle on the cross. The Old Testament anticipation of a deliverer was satisfied in the person of Christ. Paul shows how Christ has delivered man out of the bondage of sin and death. The Passover, for example, is made new in the Lord's Supper. Paul draws a beautiful parallel between the deliverance out of Egypt and our deliverance in Christ.

From what are we delivered? To what are we delivered? Paul speaks with clarity to both the Jew and the Greek. The Jews sought deliverance from slavery and bondage by the oppressor. They wanted deliverance to freedom. Paul points out that bondage to sin and death separates man from God. The deliverer, Christ,

has conquered both sin and death, and by faith man
can share in his victory. That is being delivered from
sin and death to righteousness and life.

Paul thinks of deliverance in three ways. Deliverance
is past event—Jesus and his cross. It is present experience—man coming by the Holy Spirit to faith in
Christ. It is future hope—the day when the new creation will be complete and consummated. This is the
work of Christ. To this end he faced and endured the
agony of the cross.

Paul also sees the atonement, the act of deliverance,
in three ways. First, God's love is revealed in the cross.
"God shows his love for us in that while we were yet
sinners Christ died for us" (Rom. 5:8). The cross
shows the lengths to which God is willing to go to
bring men back into a right relationship with him.
"God is love"—that was strange to the ears of those
who heard Paul preach. The Jew had understood God
as a God of wrath and vengeance, of justice and law.
God showed his love with a cross. This is the length
to which God will go—the cross. This is how much
God cares, how much he wants us back as his children.

But, this is not enough, nor is it all. God also is just.
Certainly God's love demands that he understand and
forgive us. Yet His justice demands that sin be punished. Love necessitates forgiveness. Justice necessitates punishment. The cross is a symbol of God's punishment of sin. That sounds more like "bad news"
than "good news" perhaps. But Paul found it a cause
for rejoicing, because he saw that the punishment had
been taken by Christ and nailed to the cross. Christ
became the expiation (the way out) for sinful man.

A third view of the atonement reflected in Paul's
thought is that the cross represents Christ's winning
battle over the powers of sin and darkness. Paul writes
that God has "forgiven us all our trespasses, having

canceled the bond which stood against us with its legal demands; this he set aside, nailing it to the cross. He disarmed the principalities and powers and made a public example of them, triumphing over them in him (Col. 2:13–15). Christ accomplished this by completing the sacrificial act of dying on the cross. When Jesus cried, "It is finished!", he put the final link in the bridge of redemption between God and man. Christ is the victor. He has stormed the citadel of Satan and defeated him. Mankind is set free, free to be bound to Christ. In the resurrection, Christ emerges as triumphant for he is *victor,* indeed. Death, the last enemy of man, is defeated once and for all. We can say, with Job, "I know that my redeemer lives . . . and because he lives, I shall live" (Job 19:25).

Paul attached a great deal of importance to the fact that he had seen Jesus. In the letter to the Corinthians, Paul includes himself in the apostolic group on the basis of having seen the risen Christ in the Dasmacus road experience. He wrote, "Then he appeared to James, then to all the apostles. Last of all, as to one untimely born, he appeared also to me" (1 Cor. 15: 7–8). Jesus spoke about this very idea when he said to Thomas, "Have you believed because you have seen me? Blessed are those who have not seen and yet believed" (John 20:29). The response of faith is not based upon tangible evidence. Rather, when faith once expresses itself, it becomes its own evidence.

Paul believed that man basically is a sinner; he is lost—alienated from God, himself, and his neighbor. No matter how hard he might try to overcome his own sinfulness, he cannot. Man is helpless against sin because he is a sinner by nature. If he chooses to sin, and keeps on sinning, he is a sinner by choice and by practice. The problem is more than just making mistakes. He is doomed, lost, alone and afraid. The victory of

Christ over sin is the only hope man has of ever getting
free from sin's bondage. The real sin of modern man
is to order his life as if God does not exist. This basic
rebellion against God and rejection of Christ is the
root of every problem in human life. In the light of
Calvary and the saving work of Christ, man can be
redeemed—bought back at a high price. It is possible
for man to be justified—declared innocent and ab-
solved of guilt. He can be reconciled—brought into
oneness with God.

Suffering

Paul sees in the cross an example that seems to
justify Christian suffering. Why does the true believer
have trouble, pain and sorrow? That question is by
no means new, nor is it easily answered. Paul says
that suffering "on behalf of Christ" is a privilege. Such
suffering is a blessing and not a burden because it is
suffering "with him." Because Jesus suffered, we too
might be made to suffer. And yet, because he suffered
for us we should be happy to suffer for him, if need
be. Since Christ experienced anguish, pain, rejection
and death, he understands our hurts and he suffers
with us. Christ does not make the Christian immune
to suffering, but he makes it bearable by his presence
and power.

It is quite likely that Paul suffered a great deal himself. We know there was some infirmity or thorn in
the flesh from which he sought release. He explained
that three times he asked the Lord to remove the thorn
from him, but it was not removed. Then he accepted
it as a "messenger of Satan" to keep him from being
too puffed up and filled with pride. We can't begin to
understand the mystery of suffering. Yet, we can take
comfort from the fact that our Savior never lets us

suffer alone. He stands by our side and takes our suffering on himself along with us. Paul points out that:
(1) suffering done in behalf of Christ is a privilege;
(2) Christ's suffering because of sin for others indicates that we, his followers, might also suffer for righteousness sake; (3) Christ's example of patiently enduring the ordeal of suffering will encourage us in
moments of distress; (4) Christian suffering is an evidence of being greatly used by God for vital service.

X

THE CROSS IN THE
MISSION OF THE CHURCH

Ye Christian heralds, go proclaim
Salvation through Immanuel's name;
To distant climes the tidings bear,
And plant the Rose of Sharon there.

And when our labors all are o'er,
Then we shall meet to part no more,
Meet with the blood-bo't throng to fall,
And crown our Jesus Lord of all.
                    Bourne H. Draper

And even if our gospel is veiled, it is veiled only to those who are perishing. In their case the god of this world has blinded the minds of the unbelievers, to keep them from seeing the light of the gospel of the glory of Christ, who is the likeness of God. For what we preach is not ourselves, but Jesus Christ as Lord, with ourselves as your servants for Jesus' sake. For it is the God who said, "Let light shine out of darkness," who has shone in our hearts to give the light of the knowledge of the glory of God in the face of Christ (2 Cor. 4:3–6).

The church lives by and for its proclamation of the good news of God which is revealed in the cross of Christ. To know Christ and to make him known is the lifework of the church. No objective takes a higher priority than the proclamation of the cross. The church does not exist primarily for itself. Strangely enough, the church that tries to save itself will die; only as the church gives its love, resources and its message of Christ to the world can it survive. Jesus made this principle very clear when he said, "For whosoever would save his life will lose it; but whoever loses his life for my sake and the gospel's will save it" (Mark 8:35). That same principle applies to the church. The ground of being for the church, therefore, is to make the redemptive plan of God known to the whole world. If the church fails to do that, she has failed miserably and completely. The task of proclaiming the gospel is one which the church cannot deny and a responsibility which the church cannot delegate to anyone else.

For centuries the question of the central task of the church has been debated, expounded, interpreted, and at times, misunderstood. While there are many ways to accomplish this task, to know Christ and to make him known must be central. This mission centers in the cross of Christ. This must take precedence over everything else in the church. There are many ways to get ready to carry out the Lord's command that the gospel should be proclaimed everywhere. Worship is both preparation for and exercise in the proclamation of the good news. Bible study, training, self-discipline and praise are essential elements in the overall task of proclamation. The church imitates the work of Christ —teaching, preaching, and healing. The church who loses sight of this centrality of mission has ceased to be the church.

Paul spoke of the church as being the body of Christ

in the world. Thus, it is to do the works that Christ did, to be the instrument of reconciliation which Christ was. Therefore, the most important characteristic of the church is to be a redemptive community. But this is possible only if the members themselves have been redeemed. The church, then, is a *body* of redeemed people with a mission.

JESUS IS LORD

"Jesus Christ is Lord" was and is the supreme affirmation of the Christian church. "Lord" is a word which carries with it a great depth of meaning, and it is a term which is significant to our understanding of the person and work of Christ. Of all the titles which were given to Jesus, the title "Lord" became by far the most widely used, the one which carried with it the most importance. With the passing of years, the word "Lord" became a synonym for the name of Jesus. In the gospel of Mark, there are only one or two occasions on which Jesus is called "Lord" (Mark 11:3; 12:37). Matthew deals with the term "Lord" by mentioning it only a few times. In Luke, there are about seventeen occasions when the title in its full significance is applied to Jesus. In the letters of Paul, however, Christ is called simply "Lord" at least two hundred times. This clearly indicates that the title "Lord" was at the very heart and center of the early church's understanding concerning who Christ really was.

The Greek word *Kurios* is open for a variety of interpretations and definitions. First, the word carries with it a sense of authority. It refers, of course, to domestic authority, such as a father in the home, and also it distinguishes the one to whom it is ascribed as the undisputed head or ruler. It also carries the idea of authority to make decisions and to express power, especially in moral decisions. The word *Lord* also carries the connotation of sovereign authority, which means undisputed or uncontested lordship. Of course, there is a mild use of the word in the New Testament. In such cases, *Kurios* could be just a normal word of courtesy and respect, such as would be used in addressing an elder or superior. The Christian community did not invent the word *Lord*. They found it already a great and noble word which was used frequently in the context of the official title of Roman emperors. By the time of Nero, *Kurios* was the standard title for the Roman emperor. It is also obvious that with the passing of time, the word *Lord* came to mean a word of divine power. Both uses of *Kurios* are evident from a study of the New Testament. It was a word which carried the idea of authority and a word which implied divine powers. Applied to Jesus, the word *Lord* took on new significance after the resurrection. It was certainly the discovery of the church that Jesus is Lord. It was the resurrection and the experience of him as the risen Lord which revealed to them that *Kurios* was the only adequate name by which Christ could be called. It is the resurrection title, the title of the Christ who lived and died and conquered death and who is alive forevermore. It is certain that apart from the resurrection the word *Kurios* would never have united itself so inseparably with Jesus. Also, the title *Lord* describes Jesus in his office as the Messiah of God. This becomes even clearer when we remember that the word *Christ* and the word *Messiah* are the same. *Christ* is the Greek for *anointed* and *Messiah* is Hebrew for the same word. The "Anointed One" is the divine King, because kings were made kings by anointing. This will give us an even better understanding of the Greek word *Christos,* if we remember that the word *Christ* was not originally a name, but a title meaning "The Messiah, the anointed one of God."

The words *Messiah* and *Kurios* are intimately and strangely connected. *Kurios* was the regular title of the emperor. The Messiah is God's anointed king, and therefore *Kurios* well expresses the majestic, imperial and royal power of the Messiah, and it is, therefore, a fit title for Jesus in his Messianic office.

This helps us to understand that there was a shift in the way the early church saw Jesus before and after the resurrection. To them he was Master, Lord, Savior—God's anointed Messiah. But all of these titles came to mean more to the early Christians after the crucifixion and resurrection of Jesus. Therefore the post-resurrection understanding of the word *Lord,* as well as all the other titles which had been ascribed to Jesus, was more significant, more intimate, and more theologically descriptive. In a sense, this explains why the passive devotion of the disciples to Jesus was turned into enthusiasm and zeal that spread like wildfire across the landscape after the resurrection had taken place. This also explains why Christ was presented and proclaimed to the world with such ardor and why the apostles faced death in his behalf so willingly. It is easy to see that after the resurrection Jesus was looked upon as truly divine Lord, the Messiah of God.

The early church proclaimed Jesus as Lord and the lordship of Jesus is significantly related to his saving work on the cross. The Apostle Paul said, "We preach Christ and him crucified." This is the attitude and the mind-set of the earliest Christian preachers. The apostles went everywhere proclaiming Jesus, the crucified and risen Lord. They saw him as divine Lord, which meant that he was regarded as Creator, Sustainer, Governor and Judge of the universe. They saw him as

God who became flesh to pitch his tent among men. He was made in the likeness of sinful flesh, yet was without sin. As Lord, Jesus was older than his mother, Mary. He made the air she breathed. He created the ground upon which she walked. He made the fibers of wool and flax that made up her clothing. How strange to realize that the Eternal Son of God became man; that the Eternal Savior King emptied himself. He actually poured himself out, emptied himself of His divinity, and became like man, in order that man might become like God. Paul states it so beautifully in his letter to the Philippians:

> Have this mind among yourselves, which you have in Christ Jesus, who, though he was in the form of God, did not count equality with God a thing to be grasped, but emptied himself, taking the form of a servant, being born in the likeness of men. And being found in human form he humbled himself and became obedient unto death, even death on a cross. Therefore God has highly exalted him and bestowed on him the name which is above every name, that at the name of Jesus every knee should bow, in heaven and on earth and under the earth, and every tongue confess that Jesus Christ is Lord, to the glory of God the Father" (Phil. 2:5–11).

The first century Christians proclaimed Christ as the one who gave up his high and heavenly station to come down to earth among men, and to die a cruel death as a man. All of this is included and intended in their confession—Jesus is Lord!

There were a variety of roles ascribed to Jesus as Lord. He is called the Mediator, the one who stands between God and the human family to represent one to the other and to mediate between the two. He brought the divinity of God within the grasp of man and he represented the humanity of the world in his reaching out to God. Paul reminds us that there is one God and one Mediator between God and men—the man, Christ Jesus (1 Tim. 2:5). Paul also declares that Christ as a mediator is more excellent than the old covenant which has passed away. He mediates on better promises and in a more lasting covenant than the old. As mediator, he is more than just a bridge between God and man; he is aggressively reaching out in behalf of God toward man, pleading for reconciliation, and he is equally aggressive as he represents man reaching out toward God, pleading for forgiveness.

Christ as Lord is seen as a prophet. Luke quotes from the Pentateuch as he ascribes the role of prophet to Christ. "The Lord God will raise up for you a prophet from your brethren . . ." (Acts 3:22). The prophet is a man to whom God has spoken, one who can see the things ordinary men might miss. He is a seer of conditions as they are against the backdrop of the perfect nature and character of God. He is one who can tell forth the whole counsels of God in the light of what he sees. The prophet is a man who is controlled and guided by God, one who has been anointed and set apart for his prophetic task. His life is not his own; he belongs to God. The prophet is a man through whom God reveals his message to the world. He is a servant of God and he is one in whom God has placed a great deal of trust and responsibility. His supreme function is to declare the will and purpose of God in an effort to turn men back to God. Christ was proclaimed by the early church as Priest. The temple held a very significant place in the religious life of the Jews and consequently the position of the high priest was both familiar and important. The Messiah in the Old Testament was never thought of in terms of the priesthood. There is only one intertestamental book which includes a picture of a priestly Messiah. This image is found in the eighteenth chapter of the Testament of Levi. The priest is one who is qualified by the uniqueness of his person and his position to intercede on behalf of man into the very presence of God. It is in this very sense that Christ, through the uniqueness of his person and his position, interested on behalf of sinful men into the very presence of God. Unlike the Levitical priest who died and who therefore could not continue in his priestly function, Christ holds his priesthood permanently and forever. Death cannot touch him and that is why for all time and beyond time he is able to save those who come to him. The role of priest is also ascribed to Christ throughout the whole letter to the Hebrews. He is pictured in Hebrews as the perfect high priest who has no need to offer sacrifice for his own sins. The sacrifice he has made needs never be made again. It has been made once and for all (Heb. 7:26–27).

Jesus was both understood and proclaimed by the early Christian community as King. Jesus was accused by Pilate of making himself a king (John 19:12). Pilate's first question to Jesus was "Are you the King of the Jews?" (Matt. 27:11; Mark 15:2). The soldiers mockingly addressed Jesus as a king, saying "Hail, King of the Jews!" (Matt. 27:29; Mark 15:18). The inscription on the placard above his head as he died on the cross read: "This is Jesus the King of the Jews" (Matt. 27:37; Mark 15:26; Luke 23:38; John 19:19). In many of Jesus' parables and teachings which were recorded by the gospel writers, Christ is frequently pictured as a king. We find abundant evidence in the New Testament that the disciples wanted him to be a militant king and to restore again the kingdom to Israel.

And yet, Christ was in every sense a king without a sword. Jesus well knew that the Messiah for whom men were waiting was to be a warrior prince and a militant king who would smash his enemies and who would mount the throne of power. It was precisely with that kind of awareness that Satan offered Christ all the kingdoms of the world if he would enter into a compromise with him (Matt. 3:8–10; Luke 3:5–8). There is no doubt that Jesus was tempted to be the kind of king for whom the nation would be waiting, and yet he refused to be the kind of earthly, militant king that the people expected him to be. Christ asserted the uniqueness of his kingship when he said, "If my kingship were of this world, my servants would fight, that I would not be handed over to the Jews; but my kingship is not from the world" (John 18:36).

Christ is King and his kingship is based on the royalty of sacrificial love and on nothing else. The only throne he could ever occupy is the throne in men's hearts. Jesus was always aware that he was the servant of God, though it was his task to announce the Kingdom. The Kingdom belongs to God. It was the aim of Christ to persuade men to respond to the love of God incarnate in himself and to enthrone God as King within their hearts and over all the earth.

We come again to the word *Kurios*. Jesus is Lord! It is in this very connection that the word *Kurios* is related to divine Lordship. And it is also in the word *Kurios* that we find a strong suggestion of the idea of Savior. Christ is often called "Our Lord and Savior" by the early Christian community. The person who is Lord, *Kurios,* is also Savior. The kingliness, the majesty and the glory exist not to take away or to destroy, but to save and redeem men.

The title Lord refers strongly to the ultimate triumph which Jesus experienced in his battle with sin and death. It is the word which is continually used in connection with his coming again—his ultimate victory. The end is the revelation of the Lord Jesus Christ from heaven (1 Cor. 1:7; 2 Thess. 1:7). It is for the day of our Lord Jesus Christ that the Christian waits. Christ's promised return and his complete and lasting victory over the realities of sin, death and destruction are promised by the very title ascribed to him. Jesus Christ is Lord!

In these various roles and titles ascribed to Jesus, we come to a clearer understanding of how the first century Christians regarded him. They saw him as completely God and completely man. They saw him as the fulfillment of every Old Testament prophecy. They saw him as the victor over all earth's sins and sorrows. He was the Deliverer, the anointed Messiah of God. The cross did not reduce the interpretation of the early church concerning Jesus. Obviously, the result of the cross was very much the opposite. The death of Christ on the cross intensified and heightened the interpretation of Jesus to the world. In fact, the crucifixion added power and strength to the proclamation of the message of Jesus Christ.

THE CROSS INTERPRETS US

The New Testament was not written by theologians. It was written by missionaries. We often miss the whole point of the interpretation of the gospel by our preoccupation with sideline issues. The writers of the gospel were not primarily concerned with such questions as "Why did Jesus deliberately go to his death?" or "How could one man's death provide salvation for the whole world?" These questions arise in the minds of theologians. But the first century Christians considered themselves missionaries. They were interested in interpreting the gospel to the world in the light of what Christ had accomplished on the cross. Their preaching took the condition of man and showed man his connection with the cross.

In our proclamation of the cross of Christ, we automatically create a condition for conviction of sin. Man cannot help but see his own unworthiness, his own shortcoming in the presence of the atoning work of Christ. The crucifixion of Christ is like turning on the lights in a room where there was only thick darkness. God turns on the lights so that man can see the condition of his own mind, heart, and life.

But the preaching of the cross does more than create a climate for man to see himself in the light of God's holiness. In our proclamation of the cross, we are actually showing Christ's effort to share with us fully in the experience of our own separation from God and our reconciliation to God. In the preaching of the cross, Christ is pictured as bearing the sins and guilt of all the human family.

We should be careful not to draw a sharp distinction between what he did in his life and in his death. For in both he encounters the force of evil and offers himself to deliver men from its power. On the cross he bore the sins of all people of all time. And he bore them on his conscience when he identified himself with sinners and voluntarily gave his life as a ransom for many. In his own death he assumes the responsibility and the punishment for all sins—collective and individual. And Jesus bears sin in the sense of bearing it away. His death on Calvary is the most potent reenforcement of righteousness in human history. It is in this very sense that Christ's death was interpreted and proclaimed by the early Christians. Every man who looks at the cross sees a direct line of communication between the cross and himself.

It is just like standing on the beach on a moonlight

night. One can see a straight path of silver running from the moon to his own feet. There is no escaping it. He might move miles in either direction along the beach, but the beam of light continues to lie directly between him and the moon. So it is with every man who looks toward the cross. He will find a similar direct line of connection between the crucified and himself. No one can look at the cross without becoming aware of the ray of love which appears to come straight from the heart of the Savior. He cannot get away from it. Christ's sacrifice has a personal meaning for him and in that love he knows his own incalculable worth to God. This is exactly the attitude expressed in the gospels and throughout the New Testament.

It is quite easy in an age of scientific advance and technology to allow human dignity and human values to diminish. With thousands of people mentally ill, economically deprived, racially discriminated against—the dispossessed of the world—the message of the cross is desperately needed. It is to the point of society's greatest need that Christ turns with keenest interest. We cannot forget that the prostitutes, the outcasts, and the helpless little children were the ones to whom Jesus gave his greatest attention. The cross is simply a climax of that kind of life. The gospel record will not let us forget that it was a no-account bandit who hung beside him at Golgotha. It was just such a one who called to him for forgiveness and Jesus took the time, while dying, to offer the promise of Paradise to a repentant sinner. He was always seeking after "the lost." And so the proclamation of the cross is a pronouncement of God's eternal interest in and concern for the disenchanted, the disenfranchised of the world. The cross puts a new valuation on humanity's refuse. Jesus deals with the socially unfit by dying for them. They are not eliminated, but redeemed.

The cross brings the concept of forgiveness into

sharp focus. It was in his death that Christ demonstrates God's demand that sin be paid for, not just condoned. But he goes beyond the demand, demonstrates the willingness to meet his own demand and to pay the price for the forgiveness of mankind. So, in reality, the proclamation of the cross is to make known the love and grace of God to all men. The communication of the life, death, and resurrection of Christ is in a sense much broader than just those facts alone. As we have tried to illustrate earlier, the cross carries many meanings and is interpreted in a variety of ways. When the Christian speaks of Christ's death, he is communicating much more than just the facts of Christ's passion. It is necessary, however, that the cross be related to man's day-by-day life situations with increased urgency and evangelistic passion. The message of the cross communicates God's truth and power to every age—even an age like ours in such desperate need. Georgia Harkness, in her book *The Gospel and Our World,* sums this up very aptly:

> What this means in conjunction with the theme of this book is that the gospel must be communicated in ways that combine honest and open thought with a living faith. 'Have you saving faith in the Lord Jesus Christ?' is the most important question any man can put to himself— or put to another. It ought to be put, both to ourselves and to others, with variety of wording as the circumstances may direct, but with a burning center. It ought to be put far more often than it is. Only so can the Church as the carrier of the living gospel maintain its existence among the churches.[1]

The cross speaks to man about sin—corporate and personal—and the need of forgiveness. The cross speaks about God's love and mercy. The cross speaks about the eternal God—who he is and what he wants to accomplish. The cross speaks about Christ, the friend of sinners, and Savior of the world. The cross speaks a word from God to social, political and economic conditions of our day. It seems obvious that people are not standing in long lines or stepping over each other to get into the houses of worship today, and yet the hearts of men are hungry for a word from the Lord. They will listen to a word about the cross.

The *kerygma* of the early church could never have endured the skepticism and ridicule of the ages had it not been rooted and grounded in the cross of Christ. In fact, it is safe to say that no evangelism will be valid and no preaching of the atonement strong and effective which does not give the cross of Jesus a central place. It is conceivable that, when the cross first happened the immediate reaction may have been to cry "Why did God not prevent it?" But Peter later explains in the first recorded Christian sermon that this, which seemed to be a tragedy, had actually happened "according to the definite plan and foreknowledge of God" (Acts 2:23). The first Christians never preached about the cross without saying "This is what God has done. This is God's purpose in action." People in Paul's day called the crucifixion a "scandal" and "foolishness." Paul refers to it as "unto the Jews a stumblingblock and unto the Greeks sheer foolishness." (1 Cor. 1:23 KJV). It is difficult to put into words the whole of God's great atoning act on the cross. It staggers the mind and challenges even the most able imagination. Men have stumbled and stammered before the glory of the cross for nineteen hundred years. And yet we have seen God acting at the cross with power and great glory. This is the hope and the redemptive word which we have to proclaim to the world, and proclaim it we must for the love of Christ leaves us no choice. We must declare to every person of every generation the good news that Christ was crucified for our sins and was raised for our justification. And because he lives, we too shall live. This, then, we are to preach. Christ is risen and they are more than conquerors who are risen with him.

NOTES

CHAPTER I

1. Emil Brunner, *The Mediator* (New York: Charles Scribner's Sons, 1952), p 504.
2. John Newman, "He Died For Me," © 1940. Renewal 1968 by Broadman Press, used by permission.
3. D. M. Baillie, *God Was in Christ* (New York: Charles Scribner's Sons, 1948), p. 192.
4. E. Y. Mullins, *The Christian Religion in its Doctrinal Expressions* (Philadelphia: Judson Press, 1917), p. 310.
5. James Sloan Coffin, *The Meaning of the Cross* (New York: Baker Press, 1952), p. 113.
6. William Manson, *The Way of the Cross* (Edinburgh: Hodder and Stoughton, 1958), pp. 85–86.

CHAPTER II

1. Leonard Hodgson, *The Doctrine of Atonement* (London: Nisbet and Company, 1951), p. 33.
2. J. K. Mozley, *The Doctrine of the Atonement* (London: Gerald Duckworth Press, 1935), p. 25.
3. Eric Routley, *Ascent to the Cross* (New York: Abingdon Press, 1962), p. 16.

CHAPTER III

1. James Kallas, *Jesus and the Power of Satan* (Philadelphia: Westminster Press, 1967), p. 24.

125

2. J. B. Phillips, *Your God Is Too Small* (New York: MacMillan Company, 1967), p. 105.

3. John Calvin, *John Calvin on God and Man,* ed. by F. W. Strothmann (New York: Frederick Unger Publishing Company, 1956), p. 25.

4. Kallas, p. 28.

5. W. T. Conner, *The Gospel of Redemption* (Nashville: Broadman Press, 1945), p. 17.

6. Kallas, p. 28.

Chapter IV

1. Charles C. Hall, *The Gospel of Divine Sacrifice* (New York: Hodder and Stoughton, 1896), p. 76.

2. D. M. Baillie, *God Was In Christ* (New York: Charles Scribner's Sons, 1948), p. 63.

3. John Calvin, *John Calvin on God and Man,* ed. by F. W. Strothmann (New York: Frederick Unger Press, 1956), p. 4.

4. Ibid., p. 41.

5. Henry W. Clark, *The Cross and the Eternal Order* (London: Litterworth Press, 1943), p. 46.

6. Alan Richardson, *The Theological Wordbook of the Bible* (New York: The MacMillan Company, 1957), p. 214.

Chapter V

1. William J. Wolf, *No Cross, No Crown* (New York: Doubleday, 1957), p. 30.

2. Emil Brunner, *Eternal Hope,* tr. by Harold Knight (Philadelphia: Westminster Press, 1954), p. 23.

Chapter VI

1. R. W. Dale, *The Atonement* (London: Memorial Hall, 1909), p. 246.
2. Emil Brunner, *Eternal Hope,* tr. by Harold Knight (Philadelphia: Westminster Press, 1954), p. 37.
3. E. Y. Mullins, *The Christian Religion in Its Doctrinal Expression* (Philadelphia: Judson Press, 1917), p. 176.
4. Emil Brunner, p. 35.
5. Augustus M. Toplady, "Rock of Ages."

Chapter VII

1. H. H. Rowley, *The Meaning of Sacrifice in the Old Testament, Bulletin from the John Ryland's Library,* vol. 33, no. 1 (London: John Ryland's Press, 1950), pp. 6–17.
2. A. B. Davidson, *The Theology of the Old Testament* (New York: Charles Scribner's Sons, 1920), p. 243.
3. P. T. Forsyth, *The Cruciality of the Cross* (London: Hodder and Stoughton, 1910), p. 187.
4. Ibid., p. 188.

Chapter VIII

1. George Buchanan Gray, *Sacrifice in the Old Testament* (Oxford: The Clarendon Press, 1925), p. 5.
2. H. H. Rowley, *The Meaning of Sacrifice in the Old Testament, Bulletin from the John Ryland's Li-*

brary, vol. 33, no. 1 (London: John Ryland's Press, 1950), pp. 6–17.

3. H. Wheeler Robinson, *The Religious Ideas of the Old Testament* (London: Gerald Duckworth and Company), p. 145.

Chapter X

1. Georgia Harkness, *The Gospel and Our World* (New York: Abingdon Press, 1949), p. 58.